BOOK THE
BUSINESS

BOOK THE BUSINESS

HOW TO MAKE
BIG MONEY
WITH YOUR BOOK
WITHOUT EVEN SELLING
A SINGLE COPY

ADAM WITTY & **DAN KENNEDY**

Advantage®

Advantage Media Group is proud to be a part of the Tree Neutral® program. Tree Neutral offsets the number of trees consumed in the production and printing of this book by taking proactive steps such as planting trees in direct proportion to the number of trees used to print books. To learn more about Tree Neutral, please visit www.treeneutral.com. To learn more about Advantage's commitment to being a responsible steward of the environment, please visit www.advantagefamily.com/green

Advantage Media Group is a publisher of business, self-improvement, and professional development books and online learning. We help entrepreneurs, business leaders, and professionals share their Stories, Passion, and Knowledge to help others Learn & Grow. Do you have a manuscript or book idea that you would like us to consider for publishing? Please visit advantagefamily.com or call 1.866.775.1696.

Visit **BOOKTHEBUSINESS.COM** to access these free resources:

 RECEIVE a subscription to the Author Success University™ monthly teleseminars wherein successful authors and book marketing experts reveal their tips and tricks for marketing and growing a business with a book

 REGISTER for a webinar led by Adam Witty: "How to Quickly Write, Publish, And Profit From A Book That Will Grow Your Business"

 COMPLETE Advantage's Publishing Questionnaire and receive a complimentary Discovery Consultation with an acquisitions editor to help you determine if your ideas, concepts, or manuscript are worth turning into a book

ACCESS ALL OF THE ABOVE FREE RESOURCES BY REGISTERING YOUR BOOK AT
BOOKTHEBUSINESS.COM

TABLE OF CONTENTS

THE BIG IDEA

9 WAYS TO MAKE REAL MONEY WITH YOUR BOOK

FAST ACTION IMPLEMENTATION, RESOURCES, AND THE ONE SECRET NOBODY TELLS YOU

THE
BIG IDEA

ONE

MAKE MONEY WITH YOUR BOOK, NO B.S.

By Adam Witty

I assume that if you have opened this book, you are a published author, or plan to become one soon. Either way, you're already ahead of the crowd. By choosing to write a book, you have set yourself among the top one percent of the global population. In a world of nearly seven billion people, a mere 500,000 people every year choose to *publish* a book. Yes, millions more write in blogs, create e-books, or self-publish. Yet few take the extra steps to write and professionally publish a book. So, congratulations. You are part of an elite group.

I'm also assuming that, when you decided to write, you began with a number of goals. Perhaps you wanted to tell your story or share a message. You may need to establish your brand or make your business a known entity. Better yet, you may be planning to grow your business and multiply your income along with it. Or, you may have pictured yourself as a best-selling author, rolling in the royalties as your books fly off the shelves.

The important thing is you've taken the first step. You are, or will soon be, a published author. You have already accomplished more than many ever will, including your competition. Now, with strategic planning and execution, I am happy to tell you your book can make all the goals I listed a reality—with one glaring exception. Let me explain.

My name is Adam Witty, and I am the Founder and Chief Executive Officer of Advantage Media Group. Advantage is a publisher of business, self-improvement, and professional development books. I'd like to begin by examining the experience of my friend and coauthor, Dan Kennedy. To date, Dan has written 10 books, and coauthored 10 more. As an author, he has established himself as a thought leader in marketing, copywriting, and business building. He has effectively created what I call the "author aura," which I define as the reputation gained after becoming a published author. This reputation is one reason why Dan is able to charge upwards of $100,000 plus royalties for sales campaigns, while picking and choosing the clients he wants to work with. It has made Dan a multimillionaire, many times over.

Dan's books also form the foundation for Glazer-Kennedy Insider's Circle, more commonly known as GKIC. In the mid '90s, Dan started with a handful of members. Over the years, his books created a steady pipeline of members for the growing organization.

Today, GKIC reaches 23 countries worldwide. More than 15,000 members pay every month to belong. Do the math and you quickly see why GKIC is a very lucrative business. And while Dan sold his share in GKIC some time ago, he continues to collect royalties and other benefits. As he will tell you, this ensures that his racehorses continue to eat very well.

Yet there is more to the "author aura" than building a business or expanding your income. As an author, you have an opportunity to create a persona that attracts true, die-hard fans. I witnessed this personally at a recent GKIC SuperConference in Dallas.

Over 700 people paid hundreds, if not thousands, of dollars to register for the conference. They shelled out $200 a night for a room and then more every day for nondescript hotel food. They ignored the inconvenience of being away from their families and their businesses. To top it off, everyone battled a late winter storm to get there. Some flew from countries around the world, and many endured delayed or cancelled flights. Still, others drove hundreds of miles through sleet and snow.

They braved all of this to come together as a group to share common beliefs and ideas. Moreover, they wanted to hear from the person who started it all, Dan Kennedy. I know how they feel. I was in that audience because I am a die-hard Dan Kennedy fan. I am a member of GKIC. I buy Dan's books. I've been in his mastermind and coaching groups. I go to his events. I tell everyone I know about him.

And thousands of his other fans do the same thing. The "author aura" has played a significant role in placing Dan among A-level copywriters, marketers, and speakers. In turn, this has provided him with an income that allows him to live life essentially on his terms.

Now, if you're thinking that Dan's results must be one in a million, or that only a lucky few reach this level of success, I would agree with you, but only to a point. There is only one Dan Kennedy, that's true. But there are countless others who have achieved their own definition of success, in their intended markets, from both a personal and a financial stand point.

Dan and I have both witnessed such success with hundreds of authors. We have worked with people from nearly every type of business and every walk of life: small business owners, entrepreneurs, professional speakers, attorneys, doctors, financial advisors, coaches, insurance sales professionals—the list goes on.

By strategically using their books, most have dramatically grown their businesses and some at incredible speed. We can list authors who have doubled their business within one year. Others attracted new contracts worth $40,000, $150,000, or more, in the span of months. We have watched authors develop new business ventures and partnerships, some completely unexpected, but all with the result of adding to the bottom line. Some are now multimillionaires, and all live very comfortably without worry. In summary, the authors who wrote their books with an end purpose in mind have transformed their businesses and their lives.

As I mentioned, these authors come from wide-ranging back-grounds. Their businesses are just as varied. Yet if you were to ask each for advice on how to make money with a book, they will give you similar, if not identical, answers. And all will tell you there is *one* exception if increasing income is your goal. In fact, they would likely say this is the *worst* way to make money with your book.

The Worst Way to Make Money with Your Book

The *worst* way to make money with a book is by *selling* it.

You heard me right. We are telling you the worst way to make money with your book is to sell it. It doesn't matter if you're selling in bookstores, other retail outlets, or online. Your chances of becoming a best-selling author, at least making an income you can live on, are slim, to say the least.

If you think we're kidding, hear us out. And prepare yourself. Statistics show the *real* story.

- The number of new books published every year has skyrocketed. Publishers in the United States alone released 316,480 books in 2010, compared to only 215,777 in 2002. Add to this figure the more than 2.7 million backlist "nontraditional" titles. These include self-published books, e-books, and reprints of titles now in the public domain. When it comes to *selling* your book, this makes for hefty competition, indeed.

- While the number of books continues to climb, overall sales are declining. According to BookScan, book sales in the adult nonfiction category have continued to drop since peaking in 2007. BookScan, by the way, tracks most book sales including those in bookstores, online (Amazon falls in this category), and in other retail outlets.

- The average number of books sold per title is surprisingly small. BookScan reports that in 2012, all adult nonfiction categories combined saw 263 million book sales. This includes topics in business, sales, psychology, self-improvement, and so on. While this may seem like an enormous number, the outlook dims when you average sales by title. In the United States most nonfiction authors sell less than 250 books per year. This amounts to about 3,000 copies over a book's lifetime.

- Very few nonfiction books will be big sellers. An analysis by the Codex Group revealed that of the 1,000 business books released in 2009 only 62 sold more than 5,000 copies.

- The chance of your book even *reaching* a bookstore shelf is less than one percent. There may be up to 1,000 titles competing for each available space on a bookstore shelf. Consider business books as an example. Today, there at least 250,000 books in print in this category. Yet superstores generally stock only 1,500 business titles while small bookstores normally have room for less than 100.

- All bookstores—each and every one—carry books on consignment. This means if your book doesn't sell, the bookstore can return the copies to the publisher with no payment due.

- Books that end up on the "mark-down" table are "remainders." In other words, 35 percent of all books published will sell at ridiculous discounts or never sell at all. Books in the latter category end up in a garbage bin.

If those statistics aren't sobering enough, we're about to provide another zinger. As an author, you'll earn an average royalty of $1.12 for every book you sell in a bookstore. A handful of authors make more, especially well-known writers. But most earn a paltry $1 or so when their book sells. Now, consider that most nonfiction titles sell approximately 250 per year or 3,000 over the book's lifespan. Multiply 3,000 by $1.12. That amounts to $3,360 dollars over several years. You won't buy much with this income stream.

Now, best-selling nonfiction authors can expect more—but not much. For example, a best-selling business book will sell between 15,000 and 40,000 copies during its lifetime. The author will have a better publishing deal than most, so he or she earns higher royalties. However, over the life of each book, he or she can expect to pocket about $30,000. Not bad, but this isn't much of an income if you want to live off royalties.

The bottom line is this: if you hope to reel in money as a best-selling author, you had better shelve that dream, and the sooner, the better.

However, this is not all doom and gloom. In fact, it's just the opposite. As we mentioned at the opening of this chapter, very few people decide to write and professionally publish a book. Plus, we know hundreds of authors who have used books to transform their business, multiply their income, and change their lives. All of these authors would heartily recommend that you put pen to paper, or fingers to keyboard, and start writing as soon as you possibly can.

However, this begs the question: why?

WHY SUCCESSFUL AUTHORS *AREN'T* BESTSELLERS

Perhaps the best way to answer this question is to ask another one. What is the end goal for your book? If you're planning to become an author, and even if you have already published a book, this is a critical question.

Here's another way of looking at it. Are you publishing to sell books in a bookstore? Or are you publishing a book to grow your business and expand your influence? If your end goal is to simply sell as many books as you can, you might as well set this book down now. The advice we have to offer won't be of much help to you. However, if you intend to use your book to generate new leads and customers and develop income for your business, we suggest you keep reading.

You see, successful authors do not view their book *as a book*. Instead, they see it as a marketing asset, the foundation for expanding their business.

Selling books matters little to successful authors. They know, with strategic planning and implementation, a book can generate several invisible income streams for any business. It can expand a client base, sell more products, and be repurposed to create a variety of *additional* products. It levels the playing field, making you an expert even among so-called big players. It provides you with name recognition in your chosen niche, elevating loyal customers to fans. It even helps you to change the lives of your readers.

And successful authors know all of this amounts to far more than any royalty check earned from book sales.

Dan and I call these the "invisible income streams" made possible by your book. As an author, you have access to several including:

- additional pipelines for lead generation

- speaking engagements

- new customers and clients through free publicity and media

- the ability to promote yourself without *selling*

- increased and higher-quality referrals

- higher returns on direct mail campaigns

- more products to sell

- omnipresence in your market

- marketing for your business, done by others

Your goal as a savvy entrepreneur and author should be to unlock as many of these invisible income streams as possible. If you aren't sure how to do this or where to start, relax. We are going to share a treasure trove of marketing tactics in this book. You're about to learn how to leverage your book to build a stronger business that weathers storms while pulling in more income. And as an added bonus, you get to make an impact with your message.

Let's get started!

THE BEST CUSTOMER IS A BOOK BUYER/READER

By Dan Kennedy

For many businesses, including mine, the highest-quality client/customer is initially attracted by a book, and is, by habit, a book buyer and reader. The habit of reading reflects many other attributes that make for a good customer: intelligence, desire to be informed, ability to process complex information, respect for authoritative sources, and thoughtful rather than impulsive decision making. I've never wanted dumb, lazy, casual clients/customers.

When people decide they want to know something about, or find a solution for, a particular need or desire, they have all sorts of choices. They can post their question on their Facebook page and solicit opinions and advice from anybody and everybody with no regard for their qualifications to opine and advise. They can use Google to find the provider in that category the shortest number of steps from their house. They can go to Wikipedia and get information that is never fact-checked or edited. There are websites stocked with content about everything from arthritis to zebra breeding. Free content about every subject abounds. Again, those who place no importance on the source can simply Google and roam. In contrast, consider the individual who uses Amazon instead of Google to find a book or books by credible authors and invests money in acquiring them. (Amazon, incidentally, is a search engine just like Google, but one used only by buyers.) Or he gets in his car, drives to a bookstore, makes his selection, buys a book or books, and returns home to read. This is a more discerning customer, more seriously committed to fulfilling his need or desire. He will likely be less price sensitive in fulfilling it too.

Further, we know this customer will read, and read lengthy material of interest to him, so we need not reduce our marketing and sales messages to a hopelessly ineffective 146-character tweet, an e-mail no longer than two paragraphs, a video shorter than seven minutes. We can deliver, as I often do for myself and for a myriad of clients in diversified fields, 8-, 16-, 32-, even 64-page sales letters, multimedia information packages with printed literature, an audio CD and a DVD, and have sincerely interested prospects invest 30, 60, 90 minutes in absorbing our full and complete presentation. We can, as I often do for clients, use direct mail to drive the prospects to an online, video-assisted or video sales letter from 20 to 90 minutes long. There are secrets about this few marketers understand, notably that the more time a prospect invests in your sales information, the more committed he is to buying in that category, the more likely he'll be to buy from you and not comparison shop, and the less price sensitive he will be. But if he can't or won't read, if he is unaccustomed to reading to inform himself, all is for naught.

THIS IS *NOT* IDLE THEORY

My own experience is profound, but there's abundant additional evidence.

In my own case the current statistics show that 16 percent of GKIC's new members[1] originate from my books, purchased in bookstores or from online booksellers such as Amazon or BarnesandNoble.com, or in digital editions on Kindle. While I won't divulge the rest of the specific statistics, I can tell you that the longevity and total customer value—namely, purchase activity over time—is much higher than that of members acquired by other means and media, and of the customers who have the longest life and highest value, well over half originated through a book.

In short, the customer who comes to GKIC from one of my books is a substantially more valuable customer than those who arrive through any other means. These are not free books used in lead generation advertising; they are real books from real publishers, sold in bookstores. But the free book offer in lead generation advertising very often outperforms any other kind of lead generation.

Consider these other examples of differential customer value:

- In a split test for a major, national correspondence school, in TV and radio ads, one group of prospects was offered a free information package, the other, a free book about moving up in the world with a better career and "the science of career development." The leads that were generated with the free book offer ultimately converted at a 3–1 ratio versus those that came from a response to the

---

1   GKIC is the membership organization of entrepreneurs that I built. A free offer from GKIC appears on page 175. I'll be referring to it in other places throughout the book.

literature offer, and the book requestors who did convert proved four times more likely to complete their courses.

- In a split test for a group of health clinics, ads offering free exam appointments were pitted against ads offering a free book and free exam. Eighty percent of the prospective patients who came via the book offer enrolled in the doctors' programs versus 60 percent of those who responded to the free exam offer, and the average, six-month dollar value of the book-offer patients was nearly double that of the others.

- When a group of financial advisors who specialize in retirement investing and make the lion's share of their money from the sale of annuities changed their advertising from free workshops with dinners to an evening with the author and a book signing, not only did the number of responses to their advertisements increase, but the average amount of investable assets of those setting appointments as a result of the evenings was also boosted.

RIGHT BAIT, RIGHT CRITTER

If you put a 500-pound block of salt in your backyard, you will attract deer, not rats. If you put a 500-pound block of cheese out there—rats, not deer.

Sadly, most businesspeople do not think strategically about the client/customer they want. They busy themselves attracting or chasing any customer they can get. This sometimes displays ignorance; they do not understand that they can control the flow, or fear—not daring to reject any—or sloth—being too lazy to do anything but broad, sloppy advertising that is usually price and discount driven. A business built with poor-quality customers, however, is a fragile thing. And, whether by strategy or default, you do choose your customers.

The book gives you two important customer selection opportunities. First, by its title, positioning, content, and "bullets" about its content and description in advertising, you can deliberately make it uninteresting, intimidating, annoying, or otherwise off-putting to the legions of people you do not view as ideal customers, and make it particularly magnetic to the kind of customer you do want. If the customer's mindset matters to you, you can create your book and book promotion accordingly. If you are a price seller and want value-conscious buyers, you can create your book and book promotion accordingly. If you want patients exceptionally receptive to alternative, nonmedical options, you can create your book and book promotion accordingly. And so on.

Working backward, the health book might be titled *Medical Lies* and subtitled *Ten Dangerous Lies MDs and Big Pharma Tell about Age*. The campaign may be: you can live to be 100, live independently, and stay off side-effects-laden drugs for life, but not if you listen to your medical doctor. The discount vacation and travel broker's book might be *Cheap Vacations They Don't Want You to Discover*, subtitled, *Why Pay More? Travel Like a King on a Bus-Fare Budget*. The campaign is all about "hidden bargains" on cruises, resorts, Disney, hotels, vacation home rentals.

In the mindset category, you'll read elsewhere in this book about a case history involving a client of mine, Matt Zagula, and my launching a series of seminars for the purpose of recruiting very high income advisors to move from their present companies to the one Matt was affiliated with and to move into a coaching program. We needed advisors earning from $500,000 to $1 million or more, and we decided to attract them by focusing on their mindset. We also wanted a particular mindset. While dozens and dozens of other ads populating their trade journals all clamored about making more money, attracting more clients, getting more bodies into workshops, we eschewed all that and talked instead about *selling at a more sophisticated level.* We believed this would intrigue and appeal to the advisor already earning a top income, an advisor with a strong ego and competitive nature, and an advisor immune to the me-too, me-too ads. We didn't want to offer the same kind of message said better; we wanted to advance an entirely different message. This birthed our campaign for the free book, *Creating Trust.* These ads, direct-mail pieces, and online media proclaimed that "everything you've been told about selling is wrong," and posited that instead of selling financial products or services or solutions, the more sophisticated advisor should actually sell trust. I'm happy to say this brought us exactly the quantity and quality of advisors we sought. In fact, it brought in "whales"—very successful advisors—that had stubbornly ignored and rebuffed other outreaches by this company month after month, year after year.[2]

So, the first selection opportunity is with the book itself.

The second is, as I discussed earlier, the attraction of someone willing to invest time in reading a book versus someone eager to skim literature, a serious prospect versus a casual one, a prospect seeking the best versus a prospect concerned with the cheapest price, biggest discount, quickest, and simplest answers.

---

2 After this campaign concluded, Matt and I killed off the promotional book, *Creating Trust,* and replaced it with a longer, more comprehensive book within my popular No B.S. Books series published by Entrepreneur Press: *The No B.S. Guide to Trust-Based Marketing,* available at all booksellers.

You *Can* Get the Customer You Want

A lot of my work with clients has to do with converting their businesses from pursuing customers to attracting them, from a selling culture to a marketing culture, to using media tools such as books to get prospects invested in time and thought and ready to buy, rather than trying to move them from "cold" (uninformed, skeptical, fearful, etc.) to "sold" by brute force. In making these transcendental shifts, focus can be taken off quantity and put on quality.

You can get the customer you want, and very often, the best way to get the best of those customers is by advertising, marketing, promoting, and putting forward your book rather than your products or services.

THREE

WHY A BOOK IS BETTER THAN ANY OTHER MARKETING TOOL

By Adam Witty

f there is one action that your business depends on for survival, it is opening doors.

Your prospects are behind closed doors, and they do everything they can to keep them sealed shut. Like everyone today, they are bombarded with messages. One estimate I've seen puts the number at 3,000 unique marketing messages every day. We find sales messages whenever we open an inbox, read the newspaper, or turn on the TV. It's no wonder your prospects wave the white flag and retreat. They turn down the TV, throw out the mail, and delete e-mail messages—anything to reduce the clutter. For most consumers, it's just too much.

Essentially, your potential customers do whatever they can to ignore your message and your invitation.

To get your foot in the door you need your prospects to make a decision. They must decide to subscribe to your newsletter, visit your business, take your call, or give up 30 minutes of precious time for a meeting. Unless you succeed in getting them to take one or more of these steps, selling anything is almost impossible. Yet getting this decision, and thus opening doors, is one of the hardest things for any entrepreneur or business owner to do.

Nearly all of the entrepreneurs I work with face this challenge and Bob Phelan is no different. Bob is an insurance risk advisor and CEO of the Litchfield Insurance Group in Connecticut. His company specializes in insurance products for businesses with 50 to 1,000 employees. He also provides a risk advisor service for commercial construction contractors.

Now, you don't have to be in the industry to know that selling insurance isn't easy. How many times do you wake up in the morning and think, "Gee, I want to go buy some insurance today"? If you're an agent, or if you have ever made it difficult for an agent to reach you, you know what I mean. As Bob himself has told me, most people view insurance as a commodity and a boring commodity at that.

To get past this issue, Bob decided to write and publish a book titled *Broke: The Broken Contractor Insurance System and How to Fix It*. His main objective was to open the C-suite doors of prospective clients. Bob needed to reach the CEOs of his target companies, but he wanted to do it as a welcomed guest rather than an unwanted pest.

How to Move Past Your Competition and into the CEO Suite

When it comes to getting a busy CEO to agree to a meeting, you can try several methods. However, few compare to sending potential clients a professionally published book along with a well-written letter. Suddenly, you are more than a salesperson with a pitch. You are an author and an expert in your particular subject. Whereas your prospect may have initially viewed your invitation as an annoyance to avoid at all costs, she now sees it as benefit. She now has an opportunity to discuss options with a trusted advisor who can potentially help her company.

Thanks to his book, Bob has opened several doors. The difference his book made is in positioning. When it comes to marketing, a book positions you in a way that nothing else can. You are no longer selling. Instead, you are providing valuable information that can help your prospect.

This paradigm shift, in part, is the result of our belief in the value of books. We consider books to be independent and authoritative sources of information. As such, books are highly valued in our society. We immediately attach a retail price to them. It may be $15, $25, $45, or higher, but we expect to pay money for a book. Whether you walk into a bookstore, or visit Amazon, we view books as objects of *value*.

Compare this with any other marketing material you or your competitors may use to generate leads. There is a proliferation of this material available to your prospects. Type in nearly any key phrase and Google will return a long list of websites. Most offer a free report, CD, newsletter, webinar, e-course, and so on. All of this content provides information that is hopefully useful for the targeted audience. Of course, its purpose is to build relationships, or in other words, to open doors.

This is sound marketing, and you *should* be doing it. But the volume of this type of information means you need another way to stand out. Now, contrast viewing free material on a website to a book delivered to your door, perhaps in a FedEx envelope. Think back to the busy CEO that Bob Phelan is trying to reach. She is sitting at her desk, fielding any number of priorities that may have cropped up that morning. When her secretary hands her the day's mail, she finds a book sitting among the letters and envelopes.

Put yourself in her chair. What would you pick up first?

Even if she doesn't read Bob's book right away, or at all, she *will* look over the front and back covers. Chances are she will glance at the table of contents and possibly leaf through the pages. And just with these actions, Bob has made an indelible impression.

Yet there is another reason why books are the key to unlocking doors of CEO suites. If you want to make an impression with CEOs, you must do so at their level. As an author, you become a member of "the club." Let me explain my point with a story.

I often attend the Inc. 500|5000 annual conference and awards ceremony; Advantage Media Group has been named to this prestigious list of fastest growing companies in America. What I have found, consistently, is that most of the speakers are authors. At a recent conference, nearly 80 percent fit this category. And, as it often goes with these conferences, many are CEOs of multibillion-dollar companies.

This goes back to my point on positioning. CEOs of multinational corporations view authorship as being so important that they write their own books. As an author, you join them on the same stage.

However, placing a high value on books, as well as authorship, is not limited to CEOs. Society, in general, holds books and authors in high esteem. Even as young children, we've been educated and trained to hold books as authoritative pieces of information, knowledge, and wisdom. This is why most people, and likely those in your target audience, do not throw books away. Our culture frowns on destroying books.

Even if you're not interested in reading a book, you may place it on your coffee table, add it to your collection, or give it away. But chances are you will never toss one into a garbage can. And this is the same for your prospects, whether CEOs in the corner office, homeowners, IT professionals, or people with aching backs. The value placed on books is your key to opening locked doors.

Let me provide myself as an example. A few years ago, I published a book titled *21 Ways to Build Your Business with a Book*. Whenever I speak, or when our company attends conferences or trade shows, we typically provide inquirers with a complimentary, autographed copy of my book rather than a brochure or some other marketing piece. We also use the book as "free bait" in much of our direct-response, lead-generation advertising. When members of our business development team speak to these prospects in follow up, sometimes as much as six months later, they often hear similar comments. "I have Adam's book sitting on my desk! I still want to write a book. I haven't forgotten about you."

Now, let's reflect for a moment on the above paragraph. Prospects are telling my business development professionals that my book had been sitting on their desk, staring at them every day, for the last six months! It is very difficult to accomplish this with a special report, DVD demo, letter, brochure, or catalog. Most simply throw those items away. But a book is different.

The One Way to Market to Prospects
without Actually Marketing

The power of a book extends beyond its perceived monetary value. Think of the marketing mediums available to you. Depending on your business, this may include a website and other online tactics, TV, radio, direct mail, ads in newspapers or magazines, and even trade shows. With the exception of purely educational content on a website, most people recognize all of them as a form of advertising. And as a business professional, you know that advertising, in general, is something every consumer tries to avoid.

For example, picture your prospects watching TV. When the commercial comes on, they sprint to the kitchen, bathroom, or where ever they need to go to take care of a top-priority need. Even if they don't have something to do, many race through commercials anyway, thanks to TiVo.

When listening to the radio, they switch stations when a commercial comes on. If scanning Google listings, they ignore ads, focusing instead on organic search results. When reading a newspaper, they skim over ads to find articles.

Now, obviously, it is possible to grab your audience's attention with these advertising methods. In fact, if you use your book in this type of advertising, it is far more effective—something we'll discuss in a later chapter. My point is when using these mediums alone, your marketing must be very smart in its messaging. If it isn't, people will do whatever they can to avoid it, with the ultimate result of avoiding your business.

By using your book, you can sidestep this problem. People appreciate receiving a copy, even if they have no plans to read it. They won't see it as an advertisement, but rather, a helpful source of information or even a form of entertainment. It allows you to fly under their advertising radar, to make a connection, and open doors as no other medium can.

YOUR PROSPECT FOCUSED ON *YOUR* MESSAGE

Now that you've opened the door and won your prospect's attention, imagine getting her complete focus on your message. By strategically using your book, you have the perfect the opportunity to do this. It is the next best thing to a personal meeting with your potential client.

Let's go back to Bob Phelan's top prospect, the CEO of a midsized company. After finding his book in her mail, she puts it in her briefcase. Later that evening, she settles into her chair and sorts through her to-read pile. Once again, Bob's book stands out, and she begins to read. Within half an hour, she decides it would be worth her time to talk with Bob.

I've already mentioned how we are overloaded with messages from e-mail, TV, radio, and online media. Your book whisks prospects away from this bombardment of information. When your prospect sits down to read, you win his or her complete attention. Buying this time is nearly impossible. Even with a top-notch sales team, it takes a lot of work just to get a half-hour meeting. Your book propels you to the front of the line by capturing your prospect's interest.

And here's another benefit. When readers open your book, it's as if you were sitting across the table, talking with them one on one. You can talk about the conflicts and issues your readers face in a non-threatening way. Instead of claiming your service is superior, which is common in advertising, you demonstrate how your philosophy, service, or product solves their problem. After reading your book, readers often come to you presold and ready to buy.

GAIN AN ADVANTAGE IN B2B ARENAS

A book may be even more important in business-to-business marketing than in the business-to-consumer arena. There are several reasons for this:

- Business products are often technical or complex. This is why it's even more important to educate your readers. In fact, business buyers are always looking for information to make their jobs easier or a task faster, or to save money. They will gladly read several sources of information, including your book, if it relates to the problem they are trying to solve.

- In the business world, a decision to buy usually involves a team. By providing a prospect company with your book, you help move this process along. Your book provides the information everyone needs, from controller to CEO. Likewise, if you focus on one-person shops, your book can help even more. After all, this person needs to address the same issues; he just has to do it *alone*. By giving your prospects your book, you provide all the information they need to be comfortable when it comes to buying.

- Anyone selling to businesses knows it takes several touches to move prospects to a sale. Normally, this could include a series of white papers, e-mails, phone calls, site visits, and so on, to convert a lead to a paying customer. However, give your business prospect your book, and now you are building a relationship. It often makes following marketing steps *easier*—if they are even necessary at all—because your prospect has already bought into your message.

Once again, we can look to Bob's situation to see how these points apply. In addition to offering insurance for businesses, Bob's company provides a risk advisory service. But what is the difference between a risk advisor and an insurance agent? Bob's book provides the answers and shows how a risk advisor can save a company thousands of dollars if disaster should happen. Explaining a concept like this can be difficult, even in a face-to-face meeting. Your book provides you with a platform to get your message across in a factual manner. Your prospects now have a clear idea of the service or product you provide and its benefits. By the time they meet with you, they are already in a buying frame of mind.

The Marketing Tool That Outlasts Any Other

Books offer another benefit that is rare in any other marketing method. That benefit is longevity. A book has the power to outlast nearly any other form of messaging. Consider an advertisement on TV or radio. In 30 seconds it's gone. E-mail messages are easily erased, if they're even opened. Trade shows quickly become a distant memory for attendees. Magazines and newspapers last until tossed into the recycle bin. And direct mail can be gone in a matter of seconds, especially if your prospect is sorting mail while standing over the trashcan.

Your message within any of these media is like a blip on the radar screen. Here one minute; gone the next.

A book stands the test of time. We develop libraries, display books on shelves, or share them with others. For many, the books they read and the books they own are a way to brag and showcase to their friends, family, and colleagues just how smart they are. The result is longevity for both your book and your message. But how long can you expect to tap into its power for your business?

- Carl Sewell wrote *Customers for Life: How to Turn That One-Time Buyer into a Lifetime Customer* more than 22 years ago. During that time span, his book was a key component in a strategy to create an empire of 18 auto dealerships. The updated edition is still available in bookstores and on Amazon today.

- Many professionals face restrictions when it comes to marketing their practice. This is why Dr. Charles Martin, a dentist in Richmond, Virginia, uses TV, radio, and print ads to market his books instead. After five years, this strategy continues to pull in not only new patients, but also people who are willing to pay top dollar for his services.

- When Jim Ziegler authored *The Prosperity Equation* in 1998, he had no guarantee how long it would last. He leveraged his book to build an automotive consulting business that has branched into speaking and information marketing. Today, the millennium edition of *The Prosperity Equation* is still going strong, having landed him a monthly column for 10 years in his industry's largest trade magazine. Talk about free publicity and visibility.

Your book is more than a marketing tool; it's a long-term asset for your business. When amortizing marketing tools over their length of use, books are typically the most cost effective. Time and time again, I've had authors tell me how new contracts, free publicity, or customers they've acquired as a result of a book have more than paid for the cost of publishing. And this often occurs within months of a book's release.

To achieve this in your business, your book must become the cornerstone of your marketing strategy, the very heart of your business. More importantly, you must commit to implementing your strategy over the long term. Using a book to market and grow your business is a marathon, not a sprint. Yes, it will take work. But if you do this, doors will swing open. You will find your dream customers and grow your business as never before. Your book will become the most powerful marketing tool for your business. In the chapters ahead, we will show you exactly how.

9 WAYS TO

MAKE

REAL

MONEY

WITH YOUR BOOK

HOW TO USE YOUR BOOK TO BUILD AUTHORITY, CELEBRITY, AND EXPERTISE

By Dan Kennedy

There is a huge secret about income that only a small percentage of top earners in every field ever figure out and use to their advantage. Most others are ignorant of it, but some see it, and instead of using it, deeply and bitterly resent it.

The secret is that the higher up in income you go, in almost any category, the more you are paid for who you are rather than for what you do.

That often isn't just, in the way most people think about justice. I can't attempt to affect how you feel about this in the pages of this book. It's a divergent and very complex discussion. It goes back in time to what you may have heard at the top of the stairs when you were a child. It has to do with ingrained belief systems, with religion, with politics, with philosophy. It begs an accurate understanding of why money chooses by itself to move from person to person and place to place. I deal with all of this at great length and in great depth in other works of mine. But here, now, I can only state the bald fact and move on. That fact is the higher up in income you go, in almost any category, the more you are paid for *who you are rather than for what you do.*

There are three keys to making yourself a powerful, magnetic, trusted, high-income "who" to any target audience or market: expert status, authority, and celebrity.

How Do You *Know* It's a Salesman in the Woods?

If you are wandering about in the forest, you will probably recognize a bear if you encounter one. You know bears are big, furry, black or brown, with snouts, and so on. You've seen photos. You've seen them on TV and in movies.

Similarly, you know how to spot a *dreaded* salesman in the woods. He has lots of brochures, maybe a PowerPoint presentation on a laptop, sales matter. He usually assaults you and tries to get you to an appointment by various stratagems. In his cubicle or office there are plaques and trophies proclaiming his sales prowess. Like bears, these sales creatures are to be feared and avoided.

You also know how to spot an expert in the woods. One of the most certain benchmarks of an expert is that he is the author of a book—not a brochure—a book. He has probably also been interviewed about his book (represented on a CD, DVD, or in an online video). There are probably newspaper or magazine or professional journals about his book. All this can be self-manufactured—and should be.

Although I have been a salesman virtually every day of my life, I have gone to great pains not to be perceived as one. I have used books, beginning very early in my career to the present, as a key means of *elevating my status* in the minds of my clientele. This is important because money follows and flows to status.

My first real book was *The Ultimate Sales Letter*, first published in 1981, and on bookstore shelves without interruption ever since. It established me as an expert in the craftsmanship of letters that sell. It directly brought me clients, but much more importantly, it elevated my status above other copywriters. People wanted to hear from and get assistance from "the guy who wrote *the* book" about sales letters, and it is not accidental that the pre-emptive word *the* is in that title. I have since written more than 30 books, with seven different publishing companies and gone to considerable effort to get them advertised and promoted, to keep them in print and distribution, and to use the expert status conveyed by being the author of each book and of an entire series of books to every possible advantage.

Back when I flew commercial—I now travel by private jet—and when I was still on the hunt for clients and business, I always had copies of my books in my carry-on. In 1985 I was in first-class, on a flight from Phoenix to Houston, and the fellow next to me struck up the usual conversation. He identified himself as owner of a Houston-based advertising agency and asked what I did. Instead of an answer or "elevator speech," I stood up, got a copy of *The Ultimate Sales Letter* book, handed it to him, and excused myself for a trip to the bathroom. Two weeks later, I was conducting a nicely compensated training session for his staff copywriters, where he proudly told them, "Today, I have brought you *the* man who wrote *the* book on sales letter writing."

One more story about that first book: the owner of a very large, fast-growing, weight-loss company with a hot celebrity endorser, a robust direct-marketing campaign, and distribution in Wal-Mart, brought me to his company headquarters to spend a day discussing direct marketing with his entire staff, followed by a second day working with his three copywriters. At the start of the first day, he told me he had given *The Ultimate Sales Letter* to everybody a week before so that they would be prepared. He then asked if everybody had read it and announced he was going to conduct a quick, impromptu quiz on the book before I got started. One guy sheepishly admitted he'd been too busy to read the book. My client instantly fired him. He said, "I've invested in bringing *the number-one expert* in this field in. If you couldn't invest an hour or two preparing, I do not wish to continue investing in you."

One interesting effect of all my books: I haven't had a personal, professional brochure about myself and my services or even a business card in more than 25 years. As a professional speaker, I've never had a "demo tape," something *all* speakers have. My books stand in better stead. They erase normal and customary doubts and questions, and replace them with respect and trust.

Almost all my client referrals have been made with books too. Clients aren't all that eager to distribute your brochures for you. But they acquire status by having a leading expert working for them. Typically, when prospective clients come to me as a referral, they report that the referring client either told them about one of my books and urged them to get it and read it, or gifted them one of my books. This is what I call the "expert status halo." People are proud of their association with an expert, be that the number-one expert on home decorating in Abilene or the number-one expert on direct-response marketing and copywriting in the world (me).

Must You Sell or Can You *Prescribe?*

Certain experts, professionals, and providers do not sell their recommendations; they have the authority needed to *prescribe.*

Authority comes from a matrix of factors, including expert status as well as environment, mindset of customer, criticality of solution, and others. If you have a stomach ache that won't go away and hustle over to the local "doc in a box" urgent care clinic, you'll probably fill a prescription he issues without question, but you probably wouldn't let him cut you open and remove an organ without a lot of questions; you would demand a second opinion. However, if your chronic stomach pain takes you from your MD to a specialist at the Cleveland Clinic, who brings in another specialist, and they prescribe urgent surgery, you most likely will sign the form, lie down on the steel cart, and be wheeled away without checking out information via Google. The solution proposed is the same in both scenarios. The difference in your reaction is entirely based on your acceptance of the authority of the person making the recommendation.

In my own consulting and copywriting practice, I often present complex projects that involve fees from $75,000 to $200,000, plus royalties, and are often more complex and require more investment than a new client has prepared himself for. I never want to have to *sell* such a thing. I have developed a thorough, carefully choreographed process to avoid having to sell my service.

The following is a brief overview: a potential client typically comes forward from my books, from a referral, from participating in a seminar, or from within GKIC membership. The potential client is prevented from contacting me via phone or otherwise and instead is required to fax me a memo describing his business and perceived needs. He first receives a written reply, usually accompanied by one or several of my books. He must then take the initiative to book a consulting day, positioned as "diagnostic and prescriptive" (at my base fee of $18,800). He may be told of or sent a book of mine to read. He has to travel to me for the day. Before day's end, he is asking me to issue a prescription—which I do. And 9 out of 10 times it is accepted. This is the power of authority.

Great GKIC members in a very different field, Jeff Giagnocavo and Ben McClure, operate Gardner's Mattress, where their mattresses are priced from $4,000 to $35,000, even while encircled by mattress stores selling at or below the national average of $700. I am impressed by and very proud of these guys. Everybody else sells mattresses. They prescribe. Often, their customers are initially attracted by their book, *What's Keeping You Up at Night?*, which can be purchased online at **gardnersmattressandmore.com**. In the store, the customer is engaged in a diagnostic conversation. For many, a particular mattress is then prescribed and taken from the showroom floor into the private Dream Room®, a room that mimics a luxury hotel suite, where the customer and spouse spend one, two, or even three hours, nap, watch TV, read, and fully, comfortably experience the chosen bed. To date, the percentage of customers who buy after trying out the bed in the Dream Room® is—drum roll, please—100 percent. This is the power of authority.

One of the GKIC members in my top coaching program is Steve Adams, the owner of twenty-one exceptionally profitable retail pet stores. In each store, there is a professional pet nutrition counselor who engages customers in a diagnostic process, to then prescribe the best customized diet and food for that person's pet. The total customer value and retention is much, much higher than ordinary stores manage. That's the power of authority.

If you want to be liberated from selling, if you want the authority to prescribe, I always advise writing and publishing at least one book.

THE IRRATIONAL REACTION TO STAR POWER

As I am writing this, there are two supremely successful TV ad campaigns you have probably seen ad nauseam: one for an herbal prostate remedy, starring former NFL quarterback Joe Theisman; the other for investing in gold, starring the grey-haired, rugged-looking actor William Devane. These campaigns are minting money with star power. I have been intimately involved in countless uses of star power, including my work with Guthy-Renker, the company that made the career of motivational speaker Tony Robbins by surrounding him with celebrities in infomercials and developed the $800-million Proactiv brand, the number-one acne treatment in America with advertising starting with TV sitcom star Judith Light and recently continuing with Justin Bieber and Katy Perry.

People react *irrationally* to celebrities and celebrity endorsements. And at all levels: NetJets sales improved as soon as Warren Buffett bought the company. Warren is a rich person's celebrity. He is not an expert in air travel safety. Viagra® was made popular beginning with ads starring former Chicago Bears coach Mike Ditka, a cigar-chomping tough guy, a man's man, but not an expert on medicine. If people were rational, it would be better to promote NetJets with a highly credentialed expert in aircraft maintenance and to promote Viagra® with a top doctor from the Harvard Medical School. But people are not rational. At Guthy-Renker, for Proactiv, Bill Guthy, Greg Renker, and their marketing wizard, Lenny Lieberman, brilliantly cobbled both experts and celebrities: the product's inventors, two women dermatologists, have been made celebrities by the TV shows, and the shows use Hollywood celebrities too.

I have used star power by association, rented star power, and manufactured star power throughout my business life, and used my books in concert with it.

A book is a marvelous tool to get star power by association. The leading economist and demographics expert, Harry Dent, frequently seen on Fox Business, endorsed my *No B.S. Trust-Based Marketing* book, and his "blurb" appears at the top of the back cover and has been used in its advertising. In my world, top speakers such as Brian Tracy and Tom Hopkins are celebrities, and they've written introductions to two of my books. Joan Rivers endorsed an older book of mine, *Make Millions with Your Ideas*. I used Donald Trump in a book promotion, by getting an endorsement from a contestant on Trump's TV show *The Apprentice* in which she says "Even Donald Trump could learn a thing or two from Dan's book."

My status as a book author is used at every GKIC major event, international conferences that draw 1,000 to 1,500 entrepreneurs. We always do a book signing, where people line up, have books autographed, and take photos with me. The staff moves them along; I have an assistant present. The signing looks and feels just as if I were a celebrity! This is important, because members like thinking of me as a celebrity with star power. The signing also sells a lot of books. My readers are proud of their association with Dan the Leading Expert and Dan the Celebrity. People often buy books and bring six, eight, twenty books to be autographed to different people— their employees, clients, peers, and friends. I frankly don't care that much about the sales of those books, but I welcome them working for me as a subtle sales force, reaching lots of people I might never reach otherwise, at no out-of-pocket cost, bringing new customers to GKIC and occasionally a client to me. In 2012 a new client who came to me directly after being gifted a book spent over $150,000 with me. A few of those each year can keep you warm all winter long.

A big part of my celebrity value to GKIC, to associations or groups that hire me as a speaker, and to clients I endorse is due to my status as an author and promotion of me as a book author. As part of my author business, I often invite selected entrepreneurs and experts into my books as coauthors or guest-chapter authors, and collect participation fees and other promotional considerations for doing so. They are eager to "pay to play," to be linked with me, and to use the books in their marketing and promotion because I have positioned myself as an expert, authority, and celebrity.

People often ask me why I have written so many books and why I keep writing books, and this is the principal reason: it is a key to making attachment to me valuable to others, whether that attachment is directly paid for "cafeteria-style," by renting me as a speaker, guest coach at mastermind meetings, coauthor, and so on, or is the glue of an ongoing relationship, as it is for me with GKIC and several other companies I have promoted ties to, such as the direct marketing software firm, Infusionsoft.

I have also gotten a lot of speaking engagements on programs where I've appeared —often repeatedly—with an eclectic collection of political, business and world leaders, and Hollywood and sports celebrities. I've spent nine years with the famous SUCCESS events (held in sports arenas with audiences of 10,000 to 35,000), and I've attended many clients' events. I often urge clients to hire celebrity speakers; at GKIC events, where we always use at least one celebrity-entrepreneur, the list has included Gene Simmons (KISS), Joan Rivers, Ivanka Trump, John Rich (Winner, *Celebrity Apprentice*) and Barbara Corcoran (*Shark Tank*). In some ways, the existence of my books has aided in securing these opportunities and, in a closed loop, these opportunities have driven book sales and made publishers eager to have me as an author. The following list (on page 56) is impressive to a lot of people, but arguably it should not influence their thinking about my value as an advisor on business or marketing matters. There is no rational link between my appearing on programs with these people and my expertise and trustworthiness as someone to tell you how to invest your money in advertising and marketing. It should not be influential. But it is.

THE TRIFECTA OF MAGNETIC ATTRACTION AND RISING INCOME

When you combine expert status, authority and celebrity, you cash in a winning trifecta ticket. These three factors, working in concert, act to deliver three very desirable benefits: you are made able to more readily attract more and better clients/customers, make selling to them easier, and make price less of an issue so that the profitability of your business improves.

Partial List Of Celebrities, Authors, Business Leaders & Others Dan Kennedy Has Appeared On Programs With As A Speaker

Political & World Leaders
President Gerald Ford*
President Ronald Reagan*
President George Bush*
Gen. Norman Schwarzkopf*
Secretary Colin Powell*
Mikail Gorbachev*
Lady Margaret Thatcher*
William Bennett*

Legendary Entrepreneurs
Mark McCormack* *Sports Agent, Founder IMG, Author, What They Don't Teach You At Harvard Business School)*
    Ben & Jerry*
    (Ben & Jerry's Ice Cream)
    Debbi Fields*
    (Mrs. Fields Cookies)
    Jim McCann*
    (1-800-Flowers)
    Joe Sugarman*
    (Blu-Blockers)
    Donald Trump

Hollywood Personalities & Entertainers
    Bill Cosby*
    Johnny Cash
    Naomi Judd*
    Mary Tyler Moore*
    Christopher Reeve*
    The Smothers Brothers
    Willard Scott*
    Barbara Walters
    Charlton Heston

Broadcasters
    Larry King*
    Paul Harvey*
    Deborah Norville

Authors & Speakers
Zig Ziglar* *(See You At The Top)*
Brian Tracy*
Jim Rohn*
Tom Hopkins*
Mark Victor Hansen*
(Chicken Soup For The Soul)
Tony Robbins* *(Unlimited Power)*
Mike Vance* *(Dean, Disney Univ.; Think Outside The Box)*
Michael Gerber *(E-Myth)*

Sports Personalities, Athletes & Coaches
    Joe Montana*
    Troy Aikman*
    Peyton Manning*
    Mike Singletarry
    Coach Tom Landry*
    Coach Jimmy Johnson*
    Coach Lou Holtz*
    Dick Vitale*
    George Foreman*
    Muhammad Ali*
    Mary Lou Retton*
    Bonnie Blair*
    Dan Jansen

Other Newsmakers
Lt. Col. Oliver North
Gerry Spence*
Alan Dershowitz*
Capt. Scott O'Grady*

Health
Dr. Ted Broer*
Dr. Jack Groppel*

FIVE

HOW TO USE YOUR BOOK AS THE ULTIMATE LEAD GENERATION TOOL

By Adam Witty

You've unlocked the door. Your potential clients/customers are focusing squarely on you and your company. Thanks to your book, they now see you as an expert and someone capable of providing valued information or a needed service. Leads are pouring into your funnel. The next step is to convert these leads to customers.

Your book will provide a definite advantage throughout this process. Since you've established credibility and expert status, your prospects are at the consideration stage. Now, your book will fill the gap for those who need more information before buying. It will also cement trust between you and the buyer. Put another way, your book will help prospects to slide down your funnel.

Brian Fricke is a financial planner who uses his book, *Worry Free Retirement: Do What You Want, When You Want, Where You Want,* to generate leads for his business. At last count, he had obtained five new clients directly from his book within the last 12 months. This may not sound like much, but one client is worth $10,000 annually to Brian. The result is $50,000 in new revenues every year. Multiply that by the number of years Brian will serve each client, and you can see how high this figure could climb.

Any business owner or professional can grow her business and income with a book. Brian is only one example. I've worked with hundreds of authors, both before and after publishing, and witnessed unprecedented growth in their many varied businesses. In spite of this variation, there are five common steps or "rules" that they all must follow to generate their version of success.

FIVE STEPS TO ULTIMATE LEAD GENERATION WITH A BOOK

1. Promote Your Book, Not Your Business

Marketing your book instead of your business is important for differentiation as well as regulation. If you own a medical, legal, or financial practice, a range of regulations often restricts what you can or cannot say in your advertising. However, there are no regulations when it comes to promoting a book. By using your book to market your business, you have far more freedom and flexibility. Your book becomes the subliminal sales tool that drives people into your office.

While regulations plague professionals, the problem of commoditization is one that haunts nearly any business. If you look through any directory, online or off, you'll find dozens to hundreds of listings for chiropractors, dentists, lawyers, accountants, repair shops, and so on, in any given city. What could possibly compel a consumer to choose your business over another?

Dan Kennedy was probably first in developing a creative solution to this problem. He essentially shifted the focus of advertising from a business to a book. Dan first tried this tactic with his client Dr. Bob Kotler, a cosmetic surgeon in Beverly Hills, California.

As Dan says, half of the population in Beverly Hills is comprised of cosmetic surgeons; the other half, patients. If you look through any high-end Beverly Hills magazine, there are at least 40 ads of various sizes promoting cosmetic surgeon practices. Unfortunately, for the surgeons, returns diminish with each additional ad. However, by advertising a book rather than his practice, Dr. Kotler immediately stood out. Consumers benefited with a guide to cosmetic surgery, while Dr. Kotler flourished with an increased patient load. This is something that almost any business can do.

2. Repurpose and Reuse Your Book

For many authors, writing and publishing a book is one of the most significant events in their life. You pour your heart, soul, finances, and time into creating something that stands for you and your business. It's a tremendous accomplishment. This is why you shouldn't stop with just writing the book.

Many authors repurpose content in their book to create a presence among their target market. This includes using books as a basis for blogs and podcasts. They reuse content to create articles for trade publications, **articles.com**, or leading blogs in their industry. Some even use their books as the foundation for a web television or radio show.

To succeed in business, you need to be in front of your audience as much as possible. With an average book, an author can create as many as 2,000 blog posts, 200 articles, and the same number of podcasts. This is definitely a cost-effective way to create the presence you need to pull in new leads.

3. Feature Other Businesses and Influencers in Your Book

You may be wondering what I'm talking about just by reading this title. Why would I suggest that you feature other business owners in a book intended to promote you and your company? I do this because this is an advanced strategy, and a powerful one at that.

For one thing, your book should include references to companies and resources that are important to you. If they are helpful to you, they are likely beneficial to your audience and they will appreciate the useful information.

However, there is also a benefit to you. When you feature businesses in your book, your counterparts will be happy to promote your book to their e-mail lists, customer lists, or to other people they know. They may want to interview you, the author, on a webinar or teleconference. They might give your book to clients/customers visiting their store or office. They win because they gain prominence by being "featured" in your book. Plus, they can provide their audience with a new source of helpful information. You win with exposure to new prospects for your business, and you essentially allow the "featured" business to do the marketing and promotion of your book for you.

4. Give Your Book Away

This step also seems counterintuitive. After working so hard on your book, why would you want to give it away? But, as I mentioned in an earlier chapter, you must ask yourself these questions: Am I writing a book to sell it in bookstores? Or am I trying to magnify my business and my income?

Another way to look at this is to determine what a customer is worth to you. Let's say one customer results in average revenue of $1,500 per year. If the average lifetime for a customer is six years, you get about $9,000 for your business. If you gain just 10 new customers from your book, you'll pocket an additional $90,000 over six years.

Now, consider the scenario of selling your book. With the average royalty amounting to $1.12, you need to sell 80,000 books over six years. Given that the average lifetime sales for business books is around 3,000, accomplishing this is a herculean task.

The lesson here is to give, give, give your book away to the people who matter in your target audience. I'm not saying that you should never sell your book, but I am telling you to use it as bait to attract top clients/customers. If these prospects should find you through other marketing efforts, give them your book to develop an understanding of who you are and the services you offer. Either way, you have a much greater opportunity to obtain a customer who will be far more valuable to your business than just selling books could ever be.

5. Let Your Personality Show

One of the most important things you can do with your book, and any marketing you do with it, is to let your personality show. Your business is about you and the unique aspects you bring to it. Even if you own a large business with dozens or hundreds of employees, your personality and values should be its foundation.

If you doubt this, think about multinational corporations such as Apple or Zappos. Both have hit incredible heights, in large part, due to the principles of their founders. Consider Dan Kennedy. He calls himself the "professor of harsh reality." Anyone who has read Dan's *NO B.S. Marketing* letter, or heard him speak, knows that he will provide his opinion, whether you agree with it or not. Yet he has hundreds of thousands of fans who sing his praises. And I've already mentioned how this has created financial independence for him.

When you inject your personality into your business, you stand out. It is an instant point of differentiation. You attract people who want to work with you because they believe in what you stand for. Will you repel some potential customers? Absolutely! But those you attract will be a better fit for you and your business.

By applying these five fundamental principles, you will generate both new and higher quality leads for your business. And to get you rolling, here are nine examples from real authors, just like you, who have creatively used their books to generate new leads for their businesses.

ROUND-UP GOLDEN PROSPECTS IN YOUR INDUSTRY

When Dan Kennedy and Matt Zagula decided to develop a coaching group for high-production financial advisors, they knew they had to sift through thousands of potential clients, scattered across the country, to find the golden nuggets. To most people, this sounds daunting. But Dan and Matt decided to do this by leveraging a book.

Dan and Matt coauthored, *Creating Trust In an Understandably Untrusting World: The Secret Desires of Today's Clients and How the Financial Advisor Can Prosper by Fulfilling Them.* The title makes it very clear who the book is for. It also hits a raw nerve. Financial advisors realize they could benefit by taking steps to creating more trust with potential clients.

When they released the book, Dan and Matt ran a full-page print ad in Insurance News Net, one of the largest trade publications for people in the finance, annuity, and insurance industry. The ad focused solely on how the book could help any financial advisor. The call to action was a free copy of the book. However, this is where it gets interesting.

Insurance News Book Review

Arguably, The Most Influential Book for Advisors Ever Written Explains How Top Advisors are Thriving in a Down Economy

WARNING: *"Your Prospects Don't Trust You, Not One Word You Say, Not Any Product You Represent"* say Dan Kennedy and Matt Zagula – authors of a bold and shocking new book titled: <u>Creating Trust In An Understandably UN-Trusting World.</u>

A recent MDRT study concluded that a "trust gap" has significantly widened over the last five years with regard to how prospects feel about financial advisors, citing that 85% of people trust advisors less today than they did five years ago. Shocking numbers and a trend that most likely will continue. **As an advisor, you have to ask yourself,** "What are you doing to build trust?"

When asked about the importance of trust, author and top advisor Matt Zagula had this to say: "There can be a big difference between what the reality of those MDRT study numbers tell us and what we, as financial advisors, want to believe is real. There's a lot of danger there and advisors better figure out how to gain back trust."

Dan Kennedy is, perhaps, the best known direct response marketer in America today, and his contribution to this tell-all book is evident in chapters like: *Don't Teach Unless You Want Teachers' Wages, Clients Brought To You, Not Just Another Salesman, A Much More Sophisticated Approach To Selling, The Difference IS Difference and A 7-Figure Net Income vs. 6-Figures.*

The idea for this shocking book was another industry first from Advisors Excel—the leading FMO in the industry. When asked why Advisors Excel felt it necessary to commission a comprehensive book on the topic of trust, Co-Founder Cody Foster replied, "It's become obvious to us that the next decade will be extremely challenging for the majority of financial advisors, and we felt that an investment into a program to help our advisors thrive while most struggle to survive was money very well spent."

Foster went onto say, "Our substantial investment in this has already proven beneficial because our top advisors have already gone through extensive training, based on the concepts in this book. The production immediately following the training confirms that financial advisors are actually in the *trust building business*—not in the business of selling insurance products. Frankly, we were a bit shocked by the significance of the results following the training. We initially offered the training to a select group of our very top advisors, and the immediate

and sustained value of this knowledge was measurable and meaningful, and the numbers clearly validated this important business discovery."

Dan Kennedy was floored when we told him we wanted to give away his best work ever created exclusively for advisors, so we agreed to only promote it in **ONE** magazine and only for a limited time.

When asked how Advisors Excel intended to use this new information, Foster reported, "We always look inward and roll out powerful ideas to the advisors who place their trust and business with us, and they get the benefit of the investment we've made here in better understanding advanced trust building through unique marketing, advanced sales strategies and persuasion training. That said, the book is just a small piece of what Kennedy and Zagula are doing with us, so we decided to make the book available to advisors outside of Advisors Excel to help them as well."

Taken back by that statement, we asked, "But won't that help your competitors?"

Foster replied, "It likely will, and that's okay. We've placed over $2 BILLION in premium this past year, and that growth was based on delivering tremendous value to advisors, so there isn't much reason to change that philosophy. It's well-known and documented that we are only interested in working with the top advisors in the industry, and we provide tremendous value to them, as evidenced by hiring Zagula and Kennedy. As great as this new program is, it's just one more value add we bring to the table. Advisors today are very smart, and they know they are paying something to "plug into" the carriers. Top advisors want and expect value for that money and our growth is testament to the fact that we understand their needs and continuously deliver that value."

To get your **FREE** copy of <u>Creating Trust In An Understandably UN-Trusting World</u>, just call the 24-hour book hotline and leave the necessary information at **1-888-896-8818** or visit **www.CreatingTrustBook.com**

If interested, people had to call a 1-800 number or visit a landing page. At either juncture, they had to answer qualifying questions regarding their licensing, annual production, and annual premium averages. Advisors falling in the category of high achievers received a "shock-and-awe" package in the mail that included the book and other items. Those who fell short still received a book by e-mail. Therefore, anyone who expressed interest received useful information.

Approximately 3,500 people made the effort to request a book. Of that total, 1,800 qualified to receive a copy by mail. Dan and Matt were then able to market directly to their target audience.

Get Top Prospects Even When Your Market Is Scattered in Hundreds of Locations

Travis Miller and Jimmy Vee are the cofounders of Rich Dealers, an agency that provides marketing, management, and productivity systems for automotive dealerships. Member dealers get a monthly suite of materials and advice to promote their business. Since each participating dealership has geographic exclusivity, their advertising is unique among local competition.

As Kennedy protégés, Miller and Vee advocate that lowering prices is the worst way to sell more cars. It strips away profits and turns the selling of cars into a commoditized business. Their system provides an easier way to sell cars while bringing in more revenue. But they needed to get this point across to dealers in over 300 markets scattered across the country.

Their first step was to author a book, *Invasion of the Profit Snatchers: A Practical Guide to Increasing Sales without Cutting Prices & Protecting Your Dealership from Looters, Moochers, & Vendors Gone*

Wild—a long title, but it gets the point across. Basically, it provides dealers with 10 strategies to sell cars without lowering prices.

Their next step was to develop an elaborate package that they mailed to all dealers in areas where they had openings. Like Dan Kennedy and Matt Zagula, they offered a free copy of their book in exchange for respondents' contact information. By doing this, they were then able to contact each prospect by phone. For Miller and Vee, talking with potential prospects is a critical next step in selling their system. By offering a book, they were able to get the high quality leads they needed.

Travis Miller and Jimmy Vee are very savvy marketers. They have tried different premiums to encourage prospects to respond to their offers. What they have found is a book out-performs a free report as well as a free 30-minute consultation. A book is their most powerful lead generating tool.

THE SECRET TO FINDING YOUR BEST CUSTOMERS

When someone buys your book on Amazon or in a bookstore, that person is not your customer. She may be Amazon's customer, or Barnes & Noble's customer, but she is not yours. At that point, you have no contact information, and no means of following up. You have sold a book, but you haven't generated a lead.

However, Dan maintains that people who buy your book in a brick and mortar bookstore and then find their way to your business, will be your best customers. The person who buys your book online and becomes your customer falls in the second-best category. In fact, these two sources produce far better customers than any other means.

This is why Dan includes offers and involvement devices throughout his books, even on the covers. The secret is to have several different offers that entice people to go beyond your book and leave their contact information in exchange for something that interests them.

There are several examples you can use, beginning with overt offers in strategically located text boxes. You can also sprinkle offers throughout your text. However, the best drivers are those with a rational and compelling reason to follow up. These offers could include:

- An assessment or test, usually located on a website, that allows you to determine how you score against certain strengths or capabilities (everyone wants to know how he or she scores against others!)

- A "go-see" demonstration such as a video showing how to do a test to determine if you need a certain nutritional supplement

- Tools such as fill-in-the-blank templates or checklists

- A free CD of your exclusive interview with a person featured in your book

These offers provide a compelling reason for readers to set down their books and visit your website or pick up a phone. They also provide a reason for sharing their contact information. Once you have that information, you now have a lead. And as I've mentioned, these leads tend to become your most involved and actively buying customers.

FLUSH OUT HARD-TO-REACH CUSTOMERS BY DOING THIS

When you are one of 263 chiropractors in your city, new customers often seem beyond your reach. This is how it felt to Dr. Scot Gray with his practice in the Columbus, Ohio, area. If you're a professional of any type, you've likely experienced the same problem. When you seem to be the same as dozens, even hundreds of your competitors, how can you possibly stand out?

Scot solved this problem by publishing a book. When I last checked, he was the only author among the 260-some chiropractors in his area. This in itself differentiates Scot's practice. Yet even the title adds an element of differentiation. *Good Back, Bad Back: The 10 Things Women Must Know to Eliminate Back Pain and Look and Feel Younger* instantly lets potential clients know who Scot specializes in working with.

However, Scot took his book a step further to find and secure new clients. He now offers seminars at hospitals, businesses, and community groups, and he uses his book to open doors. His book makes it easy to approach these organizations because it provides a reason why he is special. He has found that organizers are more likely to host a seminar featuring his book, rather than featuring him talking about back pain.

Scot usually provides his lectures at no cost. In fact, he offers his book as a free bonus to encourage people to attend. He told me that many people come primarily to get their free copy. However, once there, his book provides the credibility that some need to make the leap and book an appointment. He recruits at least one new patient at every outing.

This is big money for Scot since one patient generates an average of $1,500 per year in revenues. As of eighteen months after publishing, Scot's practice had grown by 30 percent, primarily with patients he would have never had before becoming an author.

Get Better Returns on This Easy Way to Generate Leads

One of the easiest, no-brainer ways to generate leads can be through your website. By offering something in exchange for your prospect's contact information, you can build a list. However, results can be lackluster, depending on your offer. So why not get the best returns possible? A book can help you do this.

I know this from personal experience. I wrote a book titled *21 Ways to Build Your Business with a Book*. It provides a variety of examples on using a book to build a business from authors who have done it. Anyone who visits our website can request a free copy. We get approximately 500 leads every year from people who do this.

So, does it achieve its purpose? I have had several Advantage authors tell me that the book was the tipping point in their decision to publish a book of their own. If you would like to get your own example of this lead generation book, visit **the21waysbook.com**. If you read it carefully, you should find ideas to use in your business.

I'd like to give you another example of generating leads by offering books on a website. Ken Hardison is an attorney and a partner in the Hardison & Cochran law firm located just outside Raleigh, North Carolina. When you visit his website, **lawyernc.com**, you will see an offer that reads: "Request your free Hardison & Cochran consumer guide today."

Since Ken's books are approximately 50 pages, he often refers to them as consumer guides. However, make no mistake; they are professionally published books. Potential clients can choose from 10 titles, each covering a different legal issue. This in itself tells the firm what each new lead is interested in, and how they should handle follow-up. With 50 to 100 requests every week, these books are productive lead generators.

A Direct Line to Your Top Prospects

Many business owners know the markets they need to pursue to generate clients for their business. However, it's one thing to know who you need to contact, and another to get your foot in the door.

Loral Langemeir faces this situation. As an information marketer and a high-end business coach, she knows exactly who her target prospects are. However, she needed a creative way to reach them. So, she mailed a copy of her book to people who would be good candidates for her coaching program. On the front cover, she added a yellow sticky note that reads: "I loved this book and figured you would like it too. Enjoy! J."

Imagine getting this package in the mail. Your first thought would likely be, "Who is J?" It could be John, Jim, or maybe, Joan. Since *J* is such a ubiquitous letter, it could be nearly anyone. Chances are high you'll be curious enough to flip through the book. You may even read it. And you may be impressed enough with Loral to visit her website, buy a training course, or join a mastermind group.

Now there is some cost to this strategy. Mailing a copy of your book, blind, to several prospects adds up. However, Loral knows that some of her clients will spend more than $30,000 in one year. She easily offsets mailing costs by acquiring new leads with great revenue potential.

Reach More Customers by Radio

Smart business owners use every means possible to find and cultivate leads. Yet this can be difficult for any business and even more so if you are trying to promote a practice governed by advertising regulations. However, you can get around regulations by promoting your book instead of your practice. And you can use a media that your competitors often ignore.

Many professionals and businesses stay away from radio ads for a variety of reasons. However, they can be a profitable lead generator especially when your call to action is a free copy of your book. As a dentist in Richmond, Virginia, Dr. Charles Martin (**richmondsmilecenter.com**) has used this strategy with great success.

So far, Dr. Martin has written five books. Note the titles of these three:

- *Are Your Teeth Killing You?: "Open Up." This Book Could Save Your Life.*

- *Don't Sugar Coat It: The Story of Diabetes and Dentistry— What They Didn't Tell You*

- *This Won't Hurt a Bit: A Consumer's Guide to Dentistry*

Each speaks to a fear that resonates with a certain segment of the public. If you have diabetes, for example, wouldn't you be interested in knowing the link to dentistry? This is why his ads offer a free book, rather than telling people to call for an appointment.

This strategy works. People who have never heard of his practice call to get a book. Even if they don't read it, many contact his office for an appointment. This is why Dr. Martin has continued to use radio ads, with an enviable ROI, for more than five years.

HOW TO MAKE SOCIAL MEDIA PROFITABLE

If you're still trying to figure out how to monetize social media, you're not alone. Yes, you can build relationships with people by "talking" with them on Twitter or Facebook. However, gaining a lead that you can send information to and cultivate directly is something different.

The trick is to drive people from your Facebook or Twitter page to a website or landing page where you collect contact information. One way to get them there is by using your book as bait. Author and fitness model, Jennifer Nicole Lee, has a creative way to attract new subscribers through her YouTube channel, Jennifer Nicole Lee Worldwide. She occasionally holds drawings for autographed copies of her book. To enter, viewers must sign up on her website. By building her list this way, Jennifer has more people who could be long-term customers for a variety of her products. This is far more profitable than simply chatting on social media channels.

Finally...Clients You Like to Work With!

If you want to have fun in your business, you need to attract people whom you enjoy working with. One easy way to do this is by highlighting your personality in your book. However, many people worry that they will drive away clients/customers.

Let me assure you, driving away some clients/customers is one of the best things you can do. Let's look at Dan Kennedy as an example. Known as the "professor of harsh reality," Dan has a reputation for telling it like it is. This turns some people off, but it also produces ardent fans. In fact, Dan's reputation has boosted him above the crowd of marketing coaches, speakers, and consultants. By standing out, he has also attracted tens of thousands of members and followers to GKIC.

This strategy works for any business owner. Financial planner Brian Fricke (**brianfricke.com**) is another example. In his book *Worry Free Retirement: Do What You Want, When You Want, Where*

You Want he included a chapter titled, *If I Ran the Country for a Day*. He admits it's a rant, but it clearly shows his beliefs and values. And new clients have commented on the chapter. Yes, he may repel some potential clients, but he attracts people who want to work with him. Brian not only gets more leads but *quality* leads as well.

I've provided several examples to give you ideas on using a book to magnetically pull in leads for your business. Now, I'd like to leave you with a final tip: begin with a goal in mind and plan from there. Ask yourself, "Who do I want to attract to my business?" This is your most important question. Your answer to this question should dictate, in part, how you write your book. And whether you're preparing to write, or have already published, this question will help you in setting up a marketing plan that attracts your ideal clients/customers.

SIX

HOW TO USE YOUR BOOK TO GET SPEAKING ENGAGEMENTS

By Dan Kennedy

I have delivered nearly 2,000 compensated speaking engagements during my career. Today, I am extremely selective, loathe to travel, and am costly to transport as I travel by private jet, so I only log five or six speeches outside of GKIC in most years. But for many years I was a true road warrior. I knew airline ticket agents and airport pretzel vendors in 20 cities by their first names, and the Marriott room service menu by heart. In peak years, I topped 75 engagements. Over these years, I've worked with event promoters in three countries, national and state associations, and corporations. I've done the Golf Superintendents Association and the National Hypnotists Guild, the giant Parker chiropractic conventions, corporate meetings for Ski-Doo, American Honda, IBM, and Pitney-Bowes, and small meetings for groups of agricultural soil fertility consultants and personal injury attorneys, and big seminars for MLM organizations such as Amway and Herbalife. I have never been booked through a speakers' bureau, nor used an agent, nor employed an inside salesperson dialing for dollars. I've gotten every engagement myself.

Fortunately, quite a few engagements came to me, directly because of my books, or more broadly because I was known for my books, newsletters, and speaking activities. I'd say about one-quarter of all my speaking gigs were booked by order taking, the other three-quarters, by hustle, often aided by my books and by use of my books in lieu of a brochure, demo tape, website, and so on.

I also sit on the other side of this table as an event planner and conference promoter myself, working with GKIC, which is, essentially, an association, and working as a marketing strategist and copywriter for seminar and conference owners in over 100 different niche industries and professions. We hire speakers. And I can tell you, most speakers *fail* to understand and to address the needs, interests, and desires of those in charge of choosing speakers.

There are three keys to getting speaking engagements because most people who can provide you with a speaking opportunity have three tasks on their plate:

One: they need to assemble a *marketable* meeting, seminar, or convention that their members or customers will want to attend. That mandates a certain mix of celebrities, of experts, of industry insiders, of familiar and of new; of general sessions and specialty break-out sessions; of education, of motivation, of entertainment. I have spoken for three hours at a dental conference about marketing, to be immediately followed by the Smothers Brothers' dinner show. On SUCCESS events, I often followed General Norm Schwarzkopf or Colin Powell, but also Bill Cosby. Most conference planners start with a "skeleton" of content categories, time slots, budgets, and other criteria guiding their search and selection. Most know they can't just put together a good conference; they must have an interesting, exciting, marketable event. Therefore, one question you need to answer, preferably proactively, but whether asked or not, is: How will you help me market my conference and motivate people to attend?

Part of that answer can be expert status, authority, and celebrity. The conference host needs to *sell you* to its audience. The more ammo you provide, the better the story about you, the more relevance to the particular group you spotlight, the easier you make it to sell you as the "amazing creature you must see," the better your chances of beating out other speakers for the slot you seek. You can obviously support this by being *the* author of *the* book on your subject and if possible, a bestselling author, a visible author, an author with "name" media credits.

Other parts of this answer are beyond the scope of this book. They have to do with the portfolio of "canned" promotional tools and direct assistance you offer to the meeting promoter, for use in the marketing of, and run-up to, the event where you'll be speaking.

Two: the planner's second task is to have a speaker people will enjoy, rave about, benefit from, and talk about or social media-ize after the fact. A buzzworthy speaker. A speaker he or she will be thanked for having. Being an author of a book plays here too. Often, the conference host's ability to buy books at deep discount to give to every attendee or to VIPs, to have a book signing luncheon or reception for certain members or VIPs, and to create a "celebrity experience" around you autographing books is a terrific added benefit. The question you need to answer, whether asked or not, is: What is *all* the value you can bring (not just making a speech)?

Three: the meeting planner's specific objectives. These vary a lot. Sometimes, the corporate CEO or organization leader gets to speak through you and people will pay heed differently than when he says the same things. My books on tough-minded time management and on sales have, for example, gotten me hired because they assert the same messages the top dog is saying but feels he's being ignored, so he sees me as reinforcement by outside authority. Sometimes a speaker is useful in setting the stage for something to be presented, for outright sale, or for consensus buy-in. We have used athletes attesting to the power of a great coach, in advance of a sales speech by someone in the company promoting the company's coaching program. A number of authors like Robert Kiyosaki (Rich Dad, Poor Dad) have often been hired to speak to multilevel/network marketing audiences because their books endorse the general concepts of being in business for yourself, home-based business, and network marketing. Years ago, a client of mine, Buster Crabbe, the actor who played Tarzan and Buck Rogers in movies and early TV, was hired as a convention speaker and then as an ongoing spokesperson by a swimming pool manufacturer because his book on fitness promoted swimming rather than walking or jogging.

The question here, asked or not, is: How will you support my chief mission behind my meeting?

Many good speaking opportunities are in meetings where speakers must sell info-product packages from the platform on which revenue is shared between the speaker and the host. This is a difficult skill, and frankly, only a minority of speakers is willing to master it. If you do, it opens a whole lot of doors. It can also be the fuel that feeds a multimillion dollar "back-end" publishing and membership business, as it has been for me—something detailed in my business plan course for speakers, "Big Mouth, Big Money," available at **DanKennedy.com/store**. In these environments, a book is toxic: it carries too low a price and is too broadly available. It can, however, be a good bonus gift with purchase of a much pricier package of audio CD, DVD, print, digital product. If the meeting planner needs the minutes he gives you to convert directly to money for him, you must be able to accomplish that and provide evidence that you can, beforehand.

When you fully understand these three tasks and communicate with those who might provide you with a speaking opportunity based on this information, you stand an infinitely better chance of getting booked to speak.

SPEAKING IN THE ALTERNATE UNIVERSE

Today, speaking engagements in media, rather than on a physical stage, abound and can be very productive—for promotion, to spur book sales, or to attract customers to you.

This alternative universe includes teleseminars, webinars, and interview-format audio CDs, typically distributed monthly within subscriptions or memberships. The info-marketing industry contains hundreds and hundreds of entities putting out one or more of these monthly interview programs, each reaching from a few hundred to a few thousand to as many as fifty thousand listeners, and most of them welcome expert book authors as guests. At GKIC we have two such programs that, combined, reach tens of thousands of listeners every month. Many info-marketers also have internet TV or internet radio programs reaching the same audiences. Many can also use the "special-event" interview with an expert or celebrity author as a means of assembling an audience to promote something of theirs to, after, or in a commercial break within the interview. I do a fair amount of these, for each new book I author. Many info-marketers will also promote your teleseminar or webinar to their lists, the equivalent of a speaking engagement, where you sell an info-product and revenue is shared.

If you are unfamiliar with the info-marketing industry, a place to begin learning about it is the Information Marketing Association at **www.info-marketing.org**.

Many national and state trade and professional associations also host similar teleseminars and webinars and put out similar audio CDs, and those that don't can be led into doing so.

Being a book author can often get you into groups and lists you would not be granted access to for more overtly promotional or sales purposes. That's the status of authorship at work. As example, I've been twice interviewed, for an hour each time, about two of my books, on the monthly audio CD distributed by a big-name real estate company to over 25,000 agents, but they have steadfastly refused being a GKIC affiliate or promoting any of my products or events. They view the book as benign. A magazine that has twice refused to sell me paid advertising because they think what I promote competes with their own businesses did do a multipage article and a bound-in audio CD based on my books, promoting my books.

Finally, there is the talk radio universe. I know two health experts, both authors of books, who get on hundreds of talk radio shows each year ostensibly to talk about their books—and most certainly *because of* the books—but who are really there to drive traffic to websites that funnel into sales of expensive home study courses, coaching, nutritional supplements, and fitness devices. One of these works two days a week, sitting by his pool, doing one interview after another, and conducts a live webinar with open Q&A every other Saturday that all the people flowing to his site from his radio interviews are invited to, and he generates over $1 million a year in income this way, rarely leaving home.

To me, these *are* speaking engagements. And they are made possible by books.

SEVEN

HOW TO USE YOUR BOOK TO GET FREE PUBLICITY AND MEDIA COVERAGE

By Adam Witty

Imagine getting over $150,000 in business from one newspaper article. This is exactly what happened to business consultant, Keith Ayers. By combining his book *Engagement Is Not Enough: You Need Passionate Employees to Achieve Your Dream* with a solid media plan, Keith has had several articles in newspapers and journals. It took only one quote from Keith in a *USA Today* article to catch the attention of a multinational company. That quote led to a phone call to Keith and a contract worth over $150,000, at last count.

Many business owners would give anything for this type of coverage. They dream of an interview with Oprah, a profile in *Business Week*, or a guest spot on CNBC's *Power Lunch*. They know the press is looking for story ideas and sources. So, they churn out press releases and articles, hoping for coverage. Yet for most entrepreneurs, their hope for publicity remains just a dream.

The reason for this is sad to say, but unfortunately true. The media doesn't care one bit about you or your business. They care only about delivering good content to their readers, viewers, or listeners. Although they get thousands of press releases every day, most of what they see is the same old thing. If you want to stand out, you have to give them something new to talk about or a great story, and preferably something that appeals to *their* audience. You can do this with your book, if you plan well.

The tips below will help you to develop and implement a media plan that generates free, yet targeted and *useful*, publicity for your business. To get you started, I've listed two steps to take from the inception of your book topic to years after publishing.

STEP ONE: MAKE YOUR BOOK ATTRACTIVE TO MEDIA

If you're in the early stages of writing a book, this section is for you. Nearly any book gives the media something to talk about. Yet some topics are more attractive than others. Here are five ways to position your book to make it more appealing to the press.

1. **Choose an evergreen topic:**

   An evergreen topic seldom goes out of style. It deals with issues that generally remain constant, year after year. Some examples include leadership, management, marketing, or hiring and recruiting.

2. **Focus on a current event:**

   As the exact opposite of evergreen, these topics tap into current, mainstream conversations. It may be a book about the recession, the 2012 election, or the Mayan calendar. However, books on current events must be used strategically, since they're like a sparkler that burns bright while current, only to quickly die out.

3. **Get extra attention at certain times of the year:**

   Adding a seasonal dimension to your topic can garner a surge of short-term press coverage. For example, one of our authors wrote a book titled *Lincoln Speaks to Leaders*. Every February, around Lincoln's birthday and Presidents' Day, this book becomes extremely popular with the press. While it gets less attention through the rest of the year, this two-month window makes up for it.

4. **Pick a controversial or unusual topic:**

   I think everyone would agree, like it or not, controversy sells. If you have a strong opinion that lands on one side or the other of a hot topic, you will get press coverage. The same applies with an unusual topic. Consider Tim Ferris and his book *The 4-Hour Workweek*. The title almost demands attention. After all, who wouldn't be curious about working four hours a week? Ironically, Tim definitely worked more than four hours a week to publicize this book. However, once the press grabbed onto the topic, it really took off.

5. **Highlight authority-based training:**

   The media gravitates to books written by authors with credentials such as specialized training in or degrees on a topic. For example, a health book written by a medical doctor is an easier sell to media.

   So, if you're still in the process of selecting a topic, consider using one or more of these elements to position your book, or even a chapter or section within it. This could go a long way in helping you to seize media attention.

STEP TWO: BENEFIT FROM THE "LOW-HANGING FRUIT" IN EVERY FORM OF MEDIA

Before you start dreaming of television appearances or an article in *O, The Oprah Magazine*, you need to ask yourself this question: "What media should I try to get?" However, before answering, you should also ask, "What would do the most to increase my business?"

Dan once told me he would rather participate in a teleseminar with 200 cosmetic dentists than have a guest spot on *Good Morning America*. The same applies with an appearance in *Entrepreneur* magazine rather than *USA Today*. His reason for this is simple. Dan's objective is to expand his business and make money. He doesn't want media just for the sake of getting attention. He wants to be where his potential customers are.

You need a real understanding of your priorities to get the most out of media coverage. To do this, you must target relevant media that deals with an audience interested in you, your topic, or your product or service. You should also be aware of all forms of media available to you. Many business owners don't take advantage of the "low-hanging fruit" when it comes to media coverage. The list below will help you to avoid that mistake.

1. Television

This is an obvious place to start, since most authors dream of being on TV. Who doesn't? So, let's begin with national television. This includes four major networks: NBC, CBS, ABC, and Fox. It should come as no surprise; this is the most difficult television medium for an author to capture. The national broadcasters cover large, broad topics. For most authors, topics are niched or specialized to a degree where they aren't relevant for national audiences.

However, your next option is community programs, especially local news. In addition, a number of cities have specialized local stations that highlight community news or events. Do not underestimate the power of these local stations. It is much easier for you to get attention here, and it could help you build momentum to get coverage by larger networks. Again, be sure the program's audience matches the target reader of your book.

> ### Low-Hanging Fruit Tip #1: Cable TV
>
> Cable TV is a great way to gain direct access to your audience. At last count, there were over 200 cable stations, many local. Most focus on specific audiences. This includes business, health, history, animals—the list goes on. The beauty of cable is you can match your topic or business with a niched audience. You'll find people who are not only interested in your topic, but in your product or service, as well. I know several authors who have had great success in building their business thanks to the promotion they've received on cable TV.

2. Newspapers

Like television, newspapers fall into national and local categories. When it comes to national papers, most people read the *New York Times, Wall Street Journal,* or *USA Today.* But unlike TV, national papers are more likely to feature authors. However, you usually get a quote or two in an article that features other experts as well. This is still great coverage, as my earlier example with Keith Ayers illustrated. But don't stop with national papers.

Be aggressive with your local news. Some states, such as my home state of South Carolina, have statewide newspapers. The next level is regional papers. For me, this is the *Charleston Post and Courier*. But let's drill down further. At the micro level, you'll find city papers or "skirts," which are a combination of a newspaper and magazine. These are even easier to infiltrate. As a local author, they have a stake in featuring you and your book topic.

Low-Hanging Fruit Tip #2: Local Media

By now, you've probably concluded that an easy inroad with the press is through local media. This includes television, newspapers, radio, even magazines. It's true that a local paper cannot provide better financial reporting than the *Wall Street Journal*. However, it easily beats the *Wall Street Journal* when it comes to featuring a local author and her tips for investing in your city's real estate.

So, target your local news first. Your chances of grabbing attention are higher. And you can use that press as leverage to get national coverage.

---

3. Magazines

From newspapers, we move to magazines. And just like our previous two examples, you have magazines at both the national and local or niche levels. At the top, we have publications such as *Time* and *US News & World Report*. From here, there are niche magazines, many of which have national distribution. Some well-known examples include *Men's Health*, *Women's Day*, and *Better Homes and Gardens*. In business, *Inc.*, *Fortune*, *Forbes*, and *Fast Company* would be top examples. These magazines have large numbers of national and even international subscribers.

If you narrow it down further, you'll find magazines that target more specific audiences. This includes publications like *Golf Digest* and *Southern Living*. Keep going and you'll find even more specialized publications such as *Cigar Aficionado, Birds and Blooms*, and *Electronic Design*.

If you check **http://magazinevalues.com/all.cfm**, you'll find 1,717 magazines listed in different categories ranging from art and antiques to travel. This site sells magazines, and I can't guarantee that everything listed is current. However, it is a great place to start if you're looking for magazines that target your niche audiences. You'll also find a fairly comprehensive list on *Wikipedia*.

Finally, there are local magazines. In my city, we have the aptly named *Charleston Magazine*, which focuses on local cuisine, art, and events. If you're an author from the Charleston area, you have a good chance of getting an article in this magazine. The same would apply in many cities.

> ### Low-Hanging Fruit Tip #3: Affinity Magazines
>
> Take advantage of affinity magazines. A perfect example is your university or college publication. Nearly every school has one, and they are actively searching for story ideas. Most would be happy to cover, or at least mention, an alumnus' achievement as an author. If the editor feels your topic is of special interest to alumni, you stand a good chance of getting a feature article.
>
> Other examples include magazines for clubs and organizations. *The Rotarian* is the magazine for the Rotary Club, which has international distribution. If you're an Eagle Scout, as I am, you receive *The Eagletter* for the rest of your life. If you belong to an organization like this, you're likely

to be featured, especially if your article provides a service for members.

Last, but definitely not least, are trade journals or industry publications. Your involvement in a specific industry increases your chances of coverage in its affiliated magazine, especially if you are a member of the organization. These magazines offer a direct line to your potential clients/customers. Plus, many are happy to get done-for-them articles. Write an article for them, and your chance of a feature is almost guaranteed.

4. Radio

When it comes to radio, you have several choices. Once again, there are national broadcasters such as National Public Radio, or NPR, as well as programs such as CBS's *Market Watch*. At the next level is local radio on both AM and FM bands. Online radio is growing rapidly with niche music services. Finally, satellite radio offers another alternative. Over 10,000 gurus, authors, and guest experts are interviewed on radio every day. Because of this, radio offers most authors the best chance at coverage. Of course, an obvious additional benefit is that you need not travel for the interview. Plus, you can be on-air almost immediately, whereas TV and print typically have much longer lead times.

Low-Hanging Fruit Tip #4: Drive-Time Radio

It should come as no surprise that I'm recommending talk radio as the best means of promoting your book. You'll find most opportunities on national talk radio shows, or local news channels. However, going one step further will increase your chances of success. Go for drive-time radio programs. Many will be more than happy to interview you if your book

> topic is of interest to their audience. Plus, your audience is more likely to be captive, sitting in a car and listening as they drive to or from work.

5. Online Media

This includes websites, blogs, social media sites, article distributors, and more. With so many opportunities, it can quickly get overwhelming. If you're not careful, your online work becomes a black hole, absorbing precious time with little return.

One way to avoid this is to devise an online media plan with this point in mind: you're not targeting specific outlets as you do with the other media examples. Instead, you are creating an online presence so media can find you. I know several authors who have had unexpected opportunities drop in their laps because someone found their book while conducting online research.

To accomplish this, you should combine a targeted plan with a keyword-rich and intriguing title. An example would be the book written by financial planner Brian Fricke. His title, *Worry Free Retirement*, resonates with many people today. It's also an easy find for reporters who are searching the Internet for retirement topics. The book's subtitle, *Do What You Want, When You Want, Where You Want*, makes Brian and his book even more intriguing. As a result, he has snared interviews with the Fox Business website as well as *Smart Money* magazine because reporters found him while searching online.

A well-thought-out plan helps too. Author and entrepreneur Chris Hurn (**504experts.com**) is an expert at this. To promote his book *The Entrepreneur's Secret to Creating Wealth*, Chris is implementing a plan that includes:

- high profile calls-to-action on his main website that lead to a landing page where he captures lead information

- PPC (pay per click) ads driving people to his website

- search engine optimization (SEO) efforts

- social media accounts on Facebook, Twitter, Google+, YouTube, and LinkedIn for both Chris and his company, Mercantile Capital Corporation

- a book promotion kit filled with easy-to-share information that users can download from his website; and

- profiles with Shelfari, Goodreads, and Redroom

Now, this list is not comprehensive. Chris is doing even more than I've listed above. Yet if you're a solo entrepreneur, it probably seems daunting. As I said, opportunities to promote your book on the Internet are almost endless. I could write a book on this topic alone. So if this list is enough to send a shiver down your spine, start simple. Begin with a website that features your book prominently on every page, as Chris does. Then, I suggest focusing on two areas where you can get sound returns.

> *Low-Hanging Fruit Tip #5: Blogging and Internet TV*
>
> The first is blogs. Bloggers are much easier to reach than national journalists and some have more readers than newspapers and magazines combined. Plus, you can approach them through two methods. The first is to send copies of your book to well-known bloggers in your niche market. Many will review your book, and provide comments or rec-

ommendations on their blog. My only caveat here is you must be very sure of your book's ability to impress.

On the other hand, you can also offer to be a guest blogger. Most blog owners welcome guest posts. It provides them with a break and their audience with some variety. The bonus is you can develop posts directly from your book, which is a time-saver for you.

Another up-and-coming opportunity is Internet TV. Check any new flat-screen TV today, and you'll find an Internet connection on the back. What's interesting is Internet TV creates opportunities for professional networks and solo entrepreneurs alike. No matter who you are, you can create high-quality content that can be easily consumed by anyone, anywhere, at any time.

If you build an audience through an Internet TV program, you'll enjoy several ways to make money, something I'll discuss further in a later chapter. However, launching a top-notch Internet TV program will help you build an audience as well as an online presence, both of which will go a long way in promoting your book. One of the top gurus in Internet TV today is Andrew Lock, creator of *Help! My Business Sucks!* at **helpmybusiness.com**.

Remember, you can easily lose productive, money-making time when working online. So, develop a plan and stick to it. Don't wander off into the latest social media site unless you are absolutely sure you will get a solid rate of return for your time. If you're at all unsure about developing the online portion of your media plan, hire a professional. It will cost extra in the short term but will save you money in the long run.

6. Events

This is something many people overlook, but events can be extremely effective, especially with local markets. Remember, events are an easy way for many community newspapers or radio stations to develop content. If you're speaking at an event, you have an excellent opportunity to get coverage, especially with city-based magazines and small town newspapers. To give reporters a gentle nudge in your direction, send a press release beforehand. This makes the reporter's life easier, and increases your chance of a feature article or interview.

> ### *Low-Hanging Fruit Tip #6: Book Reviewers*
>
> Book reviews can be a shot in the arm for your marketing. While there are a number of reviewers to choose from, I recommend Kirkus Discoveries at **kirkusreviews.com**. You'll usually pay $400 to $600 for a review, but a good outcome from this organization definitely gets the attention of journalists.

Take a close look at all of these media opportunities and choose the methods that allow you to reach *your* target audience. Don't worry about national media, at least to start, and begin with the low-hanging fruit. By doing this, you can develop a media strategy that works for your business. Now, here are five additional tips to help you pull everything together.

Five Tips to Get the Media Attention You Deserve

1. Give Your Book Away

I've mentioned this earlier, and it's just as important here. Give free copies of your book to journalists, producers, bloggers, reviewers, or anyone who may be a key influencer with your audience. This is often the critical push to get the media ball rolling.

2. Get Endorsements Early On

You should collect endorsements for your book before you finish writing. Begin by asking people that your audience may recognize but go for bigger names as well. If asked, provide a sample endorsement that your endorsers can edit. Also, as soon as your book is published, send free copies to key influencers. Ask them to write reviews for your book on Amazon and other sites.

3. Build Momentum by Starting Small

One of the easiest ways to get the ball rolling is to start small. Begin locally or with small niche media channels. Any coverage you get will be an endorsement for the bigger players. It can also give you practice and build your confidence. For example, if you've never been on TV before, start with the local affiliate instead of NBC *Nightly News*. Even if you have complete confidence in talking with reporters, features with small outlets will still help you reach media at the national level.

4. Get More Publicity as Time Goes On

I can't put it more bluntly than this: getting free publicity for your book is a marathon, not a sprint. When it comes to getting media coverage for your book, you have to be in it for the long haul. The good news is, most books will be just as relevant in the future, as they are now. This means media will have just as much interest in covering your book two years from now as they do today.

Don't make the mistake of thinking your media window slams shut after a short period. Many authors try to do 500 things in the first month or two. If they don't get a pile of hits right away, they feel it is all for nothing. You need to develop the mentality of a marathoner. Plan to do many things, but do them one at a time, over a long period. Follow a plan and take at least one step every day. Do this, and you will get publicity for your book.

5. Leap to the Front with a Killer Press Kit

Journalists and producers handle multiple media requests every day. With all things being equal, you leap to the top of the pack if you make their job easier. One way to do this is with a well-thought-out press kit.

SUCCESS STORIES FROM
ENTREPRENEURS JUST LIKE YOU

I've provided you with a lot of information on how to get the most out of free publicity and media with your book. Now, I would like to give you some inspiration from business owners who have actually done it. We began this chapter with the story of Keith Ayers' success after a major company spotted his quotes in *USA Today*. I want to end it with more examples that you can use in your business.

How an Article in a Local Newspaper
Led to an Unexpected Contract

This example illustrates how a series of simple steps can result in new business. Steve Clark is a sales coach and author of *Profitable Persuasion: Proven Strategies for Sales and Management Success*. After publishing his book, he sent free copies to several publications, including the editor of his local newspaper. The paper ran a story in the business section, which caught the attention of the chamber of commerce. The chamber then asked Steve to speak at a business luncheon. One of the attendees was so impressed he hired Steve to work with his company. The result was a $45,000 contract, made possible by a series of steps that began with giving a local editor a copy of his book.

Become a Media Spokesperson
for a National Newspaper

As a former trader on Wall Street, Linda Franklin had no idea where she would land after walking away from her high-paying but stressful job. As time went on, she knew her passion lay in helping women live a full life, no matter what their age. She decided to write a book, *Don't Ever Call Me Ma'am: The Real Cougar Woman's Handbook*.

Like other successful authors, Linda mailed copies to editors at several newspapers including the *New York Times*. When the paper decided to run an article on the older woman-younger man relationship dynamic, Linda was an obvious choice as an expert. Several of Linda's quotes appeared in this article, and the *New York Times* continues to use her as a spokesperson for various topics relating to women over 40.

INCREASED BUSINESS FOR SYNDICATED COLUMNISTS

Legal news analyst for several news stations: John Patrick Dolan is a California criminal attorney who published his first book, *Negotiate like the Pros*, over 20 years ago. He has used this book through the years to build credibility and expert status with the media. Although there are several capable lawyers the media could work with, John's book provides the positioning they need to make him a commentator. He has appeared on networks such as Fox News, MSNBC, CNN, as well as several local channels where he provides commentary on high-profile court cases.

Syndicated column builds a consulting business: Jim Ziegler is proof that you don't need to work with the national press to build your business. Jim is a business consultant, primarily for automotive dealers. Years ago, he sent a copy of his book *The Prosperity Equation* to the editor of *Dealer Magazine*, the largest publication for automotive dealerships in the country. The editor liked his book, and invited Jim to write an editorial for the next issue. The editorial was a hit, so he asked Jim to write a regular monthly column.

As a result, if you flipped through the pages of *Dealer Magazine*, you'd find Jim's two-page column, "Dealer Advocate", in every issue. At the bottom of each column, you'd also see Jim's contact information, aimed at automotive dealers, the very people who hire him.

Jim will tell you that no one knows who he is outside the automotive industry. However, inside this industry, Jim is a rock star. Remember these words. Most authors spend far too much time trying to become a celebrity outside their industry. This is hard work, and success is almost impossible. Instead, focus on being a rock star within your industry.

EVEN A CELEBRITY CAN INCREASE
BUSINESS WITH A BOOK

If you're a baseball fan, you will likely recognize Steve Sax. Steve is a five-time All-Star and 2-time World Series Champion who played second base during a career that spanned 18 years. After retiring from the game, he became a commentator for ESPN and Fox Sports' *Prime Time*. In addition, he was a guest star on several television shows including *Sabrina the Teenage Witch, Naked Truth, Who's the Boss,* and *Sunset Beach*. He has appeared on *Good Morning America*, the *Howard Stern Show, Hannity and Combs,* and *Late Night with David Letterman*. He was also featured on *The Simpsons*. He even had a supporting role in the feature film, *Ground Control*, with Keifer Sutherland.

I would say this is an impressive list. So you might wonder why Steve decided to write a book to promote his speaking business. Yet he recently told me that his book *Shift: Change Your Mindset and Change Your World* has provided the legitimacy and free publicity he needs to move his speaking business forward. Even a celebrity benefits by becoming an author.

These are just a handful of examples from the hundreds of authors I have worked with. I hope you will use their stories as inspiration when developing and executing your marketing plan.

EIGHT

HOW TO USE YOUR BOOK IN PERSONAL SELLING

By Dan Kennedy

s I've said elsewhere, it's very beneficial *not* to be thought of as a salesman—and your book or books can be the golden master key to alternative, more advantageous positioning. Consider this: a friend calls to invite you to a dinner party. Which sounds better, that a fascinating author, the man who wrote the book about "X" will be there or a salesman will be there?

Beyond that, there are *four specific spots where the right book can be beneficial to the person who ultimately makes a sale nose to nose, toes to toes, person to person, in home or office,* such as insurance and financial professionals, chiropractors and dentists, cosmetic surgeons, dermatologists, interior decorators and home remodelers, landscape contractors, business consultants, software sales representatives, business bankers, and on and on. The four spots are:

- before the sale

- at and during the sale

- after the sale

- to facilitate referrals

So, one by one ...

1. Before the Sale

The most stressful sales experience—for salesperson and prospect alike—is when the prospect is poorly prepared or entirely "cold." The prospect is afraid, on guard, skeptical, cautious, and ill informed, so he can't even confidently ask intelligent questions and therefore either raises uninformed objections, can't see past the price, or just clams up. The salesperson is often hurried, overly aggressive, and anxious. All this is transformed when a salesperson has positioned himself in advance as an expert, an authority, and a celebrity, and the prospect has a basis for understanding the points the salesperson is going to make. For this, it's hard to beat a book, solo or in the context of what I call a complete Shock 'n Awe Package with other media. I always deliberately delay even an initial telephone conversation, let alone an actual selling situation, until a prospect can be sent—by mail or Federal Express—such a package or at least a book, and be given a chance to review it. I teach clients in diverse businesses and professional practices to do the same.

But even if you insist on being a "cold-call cowboy," as I once was some 35 or so years ago, your book can be a better ice breaker than a business card, brochure, or tin of cookies. In 1978, freshly relocated to Phoenix, I would walk into real-estate offices, insurance offices, car dealerships, and so on, and ask to see the sales manager, to discuss my speaking—for free—at their next sales meeting. It was dumb and primitive, but at the time I was a bit dumb, and I had more time on my hands than I did money, so shoe-leather marketing was the order of the day. I quickly discovered that handing the gatekeeper a copy of my book to take into the walled-off manager too busy to see any salesmen dropping by worked a whole lot better than handing over a trifold brochure. And when necessary, I left the book with a handwritten note, which generated return calls; leaving sales literature did not. By the way, I did over 100 of these free speeches, most booked by door knocking and cold calling, and I earned six figures doing it, making it possible to never do it again.

2. During the Sale

During the sales conversation/presentation, the book can be referred to. This is an interesting phenomenon. I first saw it done with rather wild abandon by the great preacher Reverend Ike, who frequently opened and read passages from his own books, just as he opened the Bible and quoted scripture throughout his long sermons, culminating in altar calls and the passing of money plates. In this way, he spotlighted his own authority and put himself audaciously on a par with the ultimate authority. I've now seen it done and have occasionally done it myself, in one-to-one selling situations. Showing a prospective client an example, case history, or set of researched facts in one of my own books is not only persuasive, but it reinforces my expert status, authority, and celebrity as a published author.

Also, if you sell in your own physical environment, you definitely want to display your authorship. There is a special purpose credenza, across from the mini-kitchen in my home office, which all clients walk past on their way in and several times during the day when fetching refreshments or visiting the restroom. It holds two tall stacks of the books I've authored, including the foreign translation editions, a Golden Quill Award from an author association, another award from American Writers and Artists, and a little Snoopy plaque that injects a bit of self-deprecating humor to the orgiastic display; it has Snoopy at a typewriter, saying, "I'm a great admirer of my own writing."

By the way, you should manage your selling environment based on what you want visitors to know about you. It is a communication and sales medium, not just a physical space.

When you visit my place, there are five things I want you to know:

1) I am a much published author and widely respected expert and authority, and a celebrity. Books and other items are displayed, framed and hung, to make that clear.

2) I am very busy with multiple clients' projects and writing. I don't need your work or money. We meet at one end of a long conference table; the other end is filled with project stacks. The outer room is a work room with projects laid out; the adjacent room is my office, with visible stacks of work.

3) I am in control of my time just as I preach; there are no interruptions all day; the phone or fax rings rarely and when it does, it is ignored.

4) I am a very serious student; there are over 1,200 books and notebooks on shelves and in stacks, rife with sticky notes.

5) I have a good sense of humor, do not take myself too seriously, and will be fun to work with. To that end, visiting my bathroom is a whimsical experience.

3. After the Sale

Buyers can be gifted autographed copies, autographed special hardcover or leather-bound editions, or complete library sets of all your books. Those failing to buy can be sent a book as part of a follow-up campaign, with relevant passages underlined and pages marked with sticky notes. Of course, publication of a new book is a reason to re-contact old, accumulated, unconverted leads.

4. To Facilitate Referrals

The reasons why most businesspeople have such low referral activity are many, most having nothing to do with client/ customer satisfaction. Achieving the maximum possible referrals is a full-day seminar subject or strategy session. But one reason is that they are never provided with a good, easy, *comfortable* way to refer business. They are asked to do awkward things such as telling their friends about the other business and acting as a "pitch man," giving out referral cards that offer new-customer discounts. By giving a client several copies of your book to give to peers or friends, you provide an easy, low-stress way for others to promote your product or service. It's even a way to give your client status because he is the client of a published author, an expert, authority, and celebrity. There is more about this from Adam in the next chapter.

IF SELLING IS HARD, YOU'RE PROBABLY MAKING IT SO

When I first learned selling, it was hard. As I gradually discovered, I was making it a lot harder than it needed to be. I can't help but encourage reading my book, *No B.S. Sales Success in the New Economy* ,for a comprehensive "system" for making selling easy.

For the most part, people love to buy but aren't so crazy about being sold. That's why they knee-jerk react to the store clerk's "May I help you?" with their "Just looking" response—even if they could use some help. For that reason, it's good to construct a process that lets them feel as if they are in charge, they are choosing, they are buying. Selling is easy when they're buying!

For the most part, customers are driven more by relationships than they are driven by product or service features and benefits, or price—particularly good customers making anything more complicated than a routine commodity purchase. They are looking for a seller they can trust. For that reason, it's good to enable them to develop trust in you as an expert and as an authority. Selling is easy when you're prescribing!

HOW TO USE YOUR BOOK AS THE ULTIMATE REFERRAL MARKETING TOOL

By Adam Witty

ne of the best sources of new clients for your business is referrals. Referred customers will spend, on average, five times more than clients you acquire through any other form of marketing or advertising. Can you imagine the implications for your business if you could increase referrals by just 10 percent?

Various studies have shown that roughly 20 percent of your clients will freely give referrals. Another 20 percent will not give referrals at all. Yet this leaves at least 60 percent of your clients who would likely refer your business, if you had a system to encourage them.

A book can play a significant role in your referral system. By using your book, you can encourage your customers to give referrals while increasing the likelihood they share the message you want prospects to hear.

And getting the right message may be more critical than you think. Dan has often told this story about one of his clients, a chiropractor with a solid business and plenty of satisfied customers.

Unfortunately, for this chiropractor, referrals were rare, no matter how hard he tried to encourage more. After doing some investigating, he discovered that his satisfied clients were actually scaring prospects away. They would describe how the doctor would contort their body in a variety of ways, all of which sounded extremely unpleasant. While his patients had the best intentions, they actually repelled people who might otherwise have scheduled an appointment.

A book solves this messaging problem. The chiropractor could explain how his process removes pain. And he could do it in a way that makes potential patients feel comfortable about seeing him. I have had several dentist and doctor authors tell me that people who read their books are better patients. They understand why procedures are important, which removes much of their fear. They also tend to be more diligent with follow up.

WHY REFERRALS MAKE MARKETING
EASIER AND INCREASE RETURNS

No matter what business you're in, your book paints a clear picture of who you are and what you do. Prospects also gain an appreciation of your values, beliefs, and personality. By the time they decide to see you, they are past the exploration stage. They already have an understanding of your style and personality. And they have chosen you because they believe you are a good fit for them. They are essentially presold before walking through your door.

This occurs because a referral is validation for you and your business. Cold prospects will have some degree of skepticism, for a variety of reasons. For one thing, they don't know you. They have no reason to trust you. And they may be afraid that you'll get their money, while providing little to no value. A referral from a friend or family member validates that you and your business are legitimate, the real deal. This is important.

Referrals are also much less likely to shop or compare. How many times have you heard potential clients say, "I'm just trying to get an apples-to-apples comparison"? They may be even more blunt by telling you, "I'm kind of shopping around." Either way, it doesn't matter. The result is the same. As savvy business professionals know, making an apples-to-apples comparison is almost impossible. When you give in to prospects who are shopping around, you create more work for yourself only to gain a customer who never really appreciates you.

The other problem with comparison shopping is that it is based on price. Customers who do this don't see your business as providing a valuable service, but rather, as a commodity ruled by price. As Dan has said, many times, if you live by price, you'll die by price.

Price matters far less to referrals. Because someone they trust has recommended you, their skepticism dissolves. They no longer think you are simply trying to make a sale. They arrive at your door with a sense of trust, even respect. This is actually another reason for their value as customers. They take less time to convert. They are ready to buy, and willing to spend more money than customers who come to your business cold.

With referrals, you get superior customers who buy more, and stay with you longer. Yet none of this matters, unless current clients/

customers refer others to your business. The secret to accomplishing this lies in your book.

THE BEST WAY TO GET CUSTOMERS TO MARKET YOUR BUSINESS

Sharing your message is only half the story when it comes to using a book as the ultimate referral tool. As I mentioned earlier, a book also encourages your customers to refer. And the reason for this lies in status.

Think of it this way. When you hire a professional, whether in health care, finance, real estate, interior decorating, landscaping, or any high-end service, you're either happy with the work, or you're not. This is why referrals for professionals have less to do with quality of work, and more to do with the person. People tend to refer professionals because they have an attachment to them in some way. It could be a great story to tell at cocktail parties. Perhaps they enjoy bragging rights because they work with you. They may like to say, "My accountant wrote the book on tax savings." And for many people, helping someone solve a problem provides them with a sense of satisfaction and accomplishment – even power. If the person they recommend also wrote a book on that solution, those feelings only intensify.

People also prefer giving or lending a book to family members, friends, or coworkers as opposed to handing them a brochure or a piece of paper with a phone number. A book actually enhances the status of the customer giving the referral, thereby making it easier to do.

With advertising cost rising and often producing lackluster results, referrals are one of your best and most cost-effective marketing tools. Essentially, your clients/customers are doing your marketing and you're getting more valuable customers as a result. This is why encouraging referrals should be a key element in the marketing plan for your book.

5 Strategies to Increase Referrals with Your Book

The first step in increasing referrals is to understand how they are coming to your business now. Analyze your client list carefully. When I recently reviewed the list for Advantage Media Group, I found that over 70 percent of our clients came to us via some form of referral. Some were direct referrals from satisfied clients while others originated from affiliate partners.

It's important to know how referrals flow into your business because you can, and should, use different strategies for different sources. So, delve into your list and get your numbers. When you have clarity, apply these five strategies in your book's marketing plan.

a) Give Your Book Away

At the risk of sounding repetitive, I'm saying this again: give your book away. Begin with your key clients, your fans, especially anyone who has already referred customers your way. Send as many free copies of your book as they will take.

Another idea is to let your clients know that you are happy to mail a free book to their colleagues or friends whenever needed. Your clients never know when a family member or friend may need your help. So whenever you interact, remind them that you will provide free books on their behalf. If needed, you can mail your book with a note from your client. This is a classic win-win scenario. Your client gets the satisfaction of providing someone with advice and a gift, with no worry of spending any time or money. You gain a targeted new lead for your business at minimal cost.

In addition to giving your book to clients, you can also use it directly in your retail business. Carl Sewell used this technique to help grow his business from 3 auto dealerships to *18*. It began in 1990, when Carl wrote *Customers for Life: How to Turn That One Time Buyer into a Lifetime Customer*, in which he details his company's Ten Commandments of Customer Service.

Carl began by leaving copies of his book in showrooms for anyone to take. He also instructed his sales people to give a copy to anyone who walked into the dealership. People appreciated the gift, even if they never read it. Those who did immediately gained a sense of Carl's strong customer service philosophy. Either way, many were so impressed they bought a car from Carl.

However, as it often happened, some people decided to purchase a different brand of vehicle. Yet they still passed Carl's book on to friends, neighbors, and family members. Sales reps recounted several occasions when potential customers came into the dealership with a copy of *Customers for Life* in their hands. They came from a referral given by a friend who had never purchased a car from the dealership. The book's message was so compelling, even nonbuyers made referrals.

Here is another idea, courtesy of Dr. Steven Hotze (**hotzehwc.com**), author of *Hormones, Health, and Happiness*. During the holidays, the staff of the Hotze Health & Wellness Center offer to gift-wrap and mail an autographed copy of the book to friends, family, or colleagues of their patients. For the patient, holiday shopping just got a bit easier! For Dr. Hotze, a valuable list of referred prospects is thereby being assembled. Last year, Dr. Hotze had over 800 requests for his book.

b) Strengthen Affiliate and Strategic Partnerships

Your affiliate or strategic partners also play a critical role in referring business to you. Your book is a perfect medium to strengthen these relationships. For example, Advantage Media Group is the official publisher of GKIC, and GKIC refers Advantage to their members. This is why we provide free copies of *21 Ways to Build Your Business with a Book* whenever GKIC has a need.

You can do this too. If you're working with affiliate partners, provide free copies of your book as bait for webinars, as swag in gift bags at seminars, or as anything else for their client base. You should also encourage your affiliates to offer a complimentary copy of your book to anyone on their lists. This is a true win-win. Your affiliates offer their lists a free book with no strings attached, which is a huge plus for them. If those who request the book decide to buy something from you, your affiliate gets referral fees while you get new customers. Strategies like these make it easy for your partners to refer new customers to you.

c) Build Relationships with Your Complimentary Service Providers

Many businesses overlook complimentary service providers when it comes to referrals. By complimentary, I mean the "pretzels and beer" relationship in which a business provides an additional service for your customers instead of direct competition. Your book provides great opportunities to increase referrals from this group.

Author and commercial real-estate broker Robert Miller is a master at this strategy. After writing *How to Negotiate Office Space: What Business Owners Need to Know Before Signing on the Dotted*

Line, Robert distributed copies of his book to several businesses. These included equipment suppliers, office furniture stores, commercial insurance brokers, lawyers, and the like.

When companies purchase new office furniture, for example, the supplier can provide his book as a gift in appreciation for their business. Even if they have already leased space, chances are they'll need to re-sign the contract in three years if they follow the industry average. Robert's book will be a helpful reference when they need it. And people who get his advice will likely choose him if they need a real estate expert.

This works for almost any business. If you're a naturopathic doctor, you can provide books to chiropractors, osteopaths, or health food stores. It could be vice-versa for any of these businesses. So think of service providers who compliment your business for both prepurchase, and postpurchase. That way, you'll catch anyone when they are ready to buy from you.

d) Consider a Licensing Program

When it comes to books, a licensing program is a coauthorship opportunity. While it isn't a traditional referral program, it can definitely result in new clients for you. Dr. Charles Martin, an author I introduced previously, does this perfectly. Dr. Martin has a thriving dental practice in Richmond, Virginia, thanks in part to his books. As I mentioned earlier, he has written four books on dentistry for consumers, with one titled, *This Won't Hurt a Bit—The Smart Consumer's Guide to Dentistry.*

Dr. Martin realizes he has an asset in these books. He knows that any other dentist in America could benefit by being an author. However, he also knows that most dentists, for one reason or another, will never invest the time and money to become an author. So, he is making the most of his books by providing dentists with an opportunity to obtain a license and become a coauthor in a market-exclusive area. Each dentist gets a book with a different cover and a chapter tailored to his or her practice and market area, but everything else is identical. As of now, Dr. Martin has eight licensed versions of his books scattered across the country.

Now you may be wondering how other dentists can help Dr. Martin with referrals. After all, they are his competition. However, Dr. Martin offers several specialized dental treatments that many dentists cannot provide their patients. Because of this, he has patients from 44 states and seven countries. For example, a sheik flew in from the United Arab Emirates to have Dr. Martin work on his smile.

When any of his coauthor dentists have patients who need highly specialized dental work, they refer those patients to Dr. Martin. This is an advanced referral technique. If you have a product or service that coauthors can help you sell, you should definitely consider licensing your book.

e) Create Custom Covers for Your Best Referral Partners

This is an easy way to encourage client-fans, especially those who are already referring clients to you. Create a custom cover for each referral partner. You can also include a letter from your referral partner on the first page. By creating something more personalized for your clients, they'll be more likely to give your book away.

Referrals will be among your best customers. In addition to being easier to convert, they are generally more enjoyable to work with. They tend to buy more and remain with you longer. And since your current customers are doing a lot of your marketing for you, getting referrals is very cost effective—if you do it right.

Your book will make it easier to acquire referrals for a number of reasons. It highlights your credibility and personality, attracting like-minded customers who refer similar people to work with you. It ensures that customers communicate your message correctly to new prospects. And it provides status for your customers, making it easier for them to refer. A referral system with your book should definitely be a part of your marketing plan.

TEN

HOW TO USE YOUR BOOK TO BOOST YOUR DIRECT MAIL

By Dan Kennedy

Y es, you should be using direct mail to market just about any product, service, business, practice, nonprofit organization or cause. Yes, in this day and age. Why? Because the most successful marketers in every category spend more on direct mail than they do on anything else and get a better, more accurately known return on investment from it than from anything else. If that is contrary to the popular myth you're familiar with, sorry.

As a quick, mind-opening exercise, here are some facts assembled for a specialized training event I conducted, called "Mailbox Millions":

- Fifty percent of consumers say *they pay more attention to postal mail than e-mail*—Epsilon Channel Preference Study, **Epsilon.com/channelpreference2011**. That means, if you insist on communicating entirely or mostly with e-mail and neglect the use of direct mail, you may very well miss *half* the sales opportunities of any given campaign or within your list.

- Twenty-six percent of consumers rank direct mail as more trustworthy than e-mail; only 6 percent ranked blogs and social media as trustworthy—Epsilon.

- Sixty percent of consumers say *they enjoy checking their mailbox and receiving mail*—Epsilon. This research indicates there is positive emotional payoff to consumers in finding in their mailbox letters and other direct mail that matches their interests, and further, the opening of "fresh" mail and discovery of interesting information and offers is an activity they look forward to! Against this, consider that 65 percent say they receive too many e-mails everyday to open them all—Epsilon.

- A fast-growing percentage of people express frustration and *resentment* at e-mail marketing, even from sources they have a good relationship with—E-Commerce Alliance Research.

- The preference for direct mail even extends to the 18–34 age group—Epsilon.

- Tangible materials such as direct mail trigger a much deeper level of emotional processing and generate more activity in the area of the brain associated with integration of visual and spatial information than any other media. This deeper emotional processing better embeds the images and ideas in the memories of test subjects—"Using Neuroscience to Understand the Role of Direct Mail," from a study by Bangor University and Millward Brown.

- Ninety-eight percent of consumers retrieve their mail from the mailbox the day it is delivered, and 77 percent sort through it that same day—USPS data, reported in Direct Marketing News, 2/11.

- In 2011 the total volume of first-class mail was depressed by 7 percent, but direct mail for commercial purposes was up 3 percent—Target Marketing, 12/11.

- More than 12 *billion catalogs* are mailed annually—Direct Marketing Association Statistical Fact Book. Question: would companies keep mailing *billions* of printed catalogs if their testing indicated they could replace them with online media?

- Investment in direct mail for advertising purposes rose by 5.8 percent from 2010 to 2011, totaling $48 *billion*—**DeliverMagazine.com**. Yes, during a recession, spending on direct mail rose. Keep in mind, huge numbers of dumb companies cut back and switched to online media, so to create this increase, the remaining users of direct mail had to *dramatically* increase usage.

- Spending on political direct mail in 2012 topped $288 million, up 11.6 percent from 2008—Borrell Assoc./Direct Marketing News, 1/12.

- "For the typical American household these days, nearly 2 months will pass between times a personal letter shows up in the mail"—USPS/Associated Press. Gee, d'ya think that just gave your personal (sales) letter an enhanced opportunity?

- "*Nothing* outperforms direct mail for new donor acquisition. Nonprofits wish that social media, websites, e-mail, and so on, could do this job as well, but so far, extensive experimenting by the entire nonprofit world has failed to come up with any way to survive and grow without *relying on* direct mail"—NP Economic Research.

- "The World's Largest E-Commerce Event!"—the Internet Retailer Conference & Exhibition—is sold via a 32-page direct-mail piece. Google uses direct mail to sell its pay per click and Google local advertising media. If business owners not willfully blind to reality, they can see that even peddlers of e-commerce and online advertising and marketing must rely on direct mail for their income. If this fact does not compel an entrepreneur to prioritize the mastery and successful use of direct mail as his own business builder, I can't imagine what other evidence would be convincing. Perhaps to believe murder existed, the denier himself would have to be killed? To deny the vital importance of direct mail as a fortune-making marketing tool is to deny concrete fact.

This is but a small sampling of the overwhelming preponderance of proof that direct mail is an essential and valuable marketing tool.

A friend of mine sold 248,000 self-published books on a health subject in 18 months, mailing a few million as direct-mail pieces, on which he pocketed over $4 million, net. *He believes in direct mail.* A client, an author of a book on personal finance that gives him needed expert status, authority, and celebrity, puts over 100,000 people a year in his "road-show" seminars and online webinars through direct mail. *He's a believer.* Another client, the author of a course on real-estate investing, generates income of $100,000 a month with an entirely automated sales process, pushing people via direct mail to a video sales letter at a website. *He's a believer.* An Arizona financial advisor fills her workshops with grade-A prospects via direct mail I developed. *She's a believer.* A member of my coaching group, the pastor of four thriving churches, creates all the new parishioners with oversized, direct-mail postcards. *He's a believer and a Believer.*

If you are still a skeptic, please do some homework at **SRDS.com**, which stands for Standard Rate and Data Service. This is the central clearinghouse of all commercially available customer and subscriber mailing lists available for rent, with size of lists, numbers added per quarter, average purchase amount, and a lot of other data. Spend a few hours looking at your category of product, service, or subject matter, and at a broader diversity of categories. Get a true sense of the epic size and scope of direct-mail commerce. It dwarfs e-commerce, but it also fuels it. Actually, no other forms of selling are disconnected from it. Of the Forbes 500 list of richest people in the world, fewer than 50 have fortunes that were not, or are not, substantially dependent on direct mail.

Can we stipulate, smart, successful marketers make direct mail work for themselves?

How Your Book Fits With Direct Mail

It's hard to trump free-book-offer direct mail to generate leads. Unlike other media—literature, brochures, even DVDs—the book is not only enticing bait, but it has gravitas; it establishes you as an expert, authority, and celebrity. And it appeals to a better-caliber prospect, as I explained in Chapter 4.

"Free book enclosed" is also a very powerful envelope gambit. The investment newsletter and health newsletter publishers, making up a billion-dollar industry, populated with a lot of independent entrepreneurs, is almost entirely fueled by direct mail and frequently sends a 6" x 9" envelope—made lumpy by enclosing a small paperback book—along with their sales letter and order form. The outside of the envelope is often printed with the image of the book cover and the words, "Free Book Enclosed." The open rate is terrific. After all, who throws out a free *book*?

Even if your book is not going to be sent or offered free, it may be that an envelope marked, "From the Author of the Controversial New Book [insert title]," will receive more favorable attention than the notation of any other return address.

If you are a B2B marketer in combat with Gap-Toothed Gertrude the Gatekeeper, whose life's purpose is trash-canning "junk" mail, you can frustrate her by delivering an actual book—with a note to the recipient in an envelope that is sealed, marked "Confidential," and taped to the book—inside a bubble-bag hand-addressed with a black marking pen. Even Gertrude dare not discard this.

A nifty trick to reach selected, very important people—Adam Witty does this—is to have your book sent by the publisher (not you) with a note indicating that the VIP was selected to receive an advance copy of a groundbreaking book in his field because he is a VIP in his industry, community, and so on. You can follow up after the ice has been broken.

KNOCK-KNOCK. WHO'S THERE?

A directmail piece—letter in envelope, a postcard, a magalog—is actually a sales representative in your employ, knocking on someone's door. Its purpose may be to prompt a call to you, to secure an appointment, to bring someone to your store or showroom or webinar. Knock-knock. Who's there?

Answer 1: A salesman representing a product.

Answer 2: A salesman representing a service.

Answer 3: A representative of an expert, authority, and celebrity, the man who wrote the book on "X."

Which fellow knocking at the door do you think stands the best chance of favorable reception?

ELEVEN

HOW TO USE YOUR BOOK FOR FAST PRODUCT CREATION AND ADDITIONAL INCOME

By Adam Witty

y now I'm hoping you agree with this statement: your book is not just a book; it's a foundation to build your business. In previous chapters, Dan and I have given you strategies for using a book to build your list, get referrals, generate leads, and a host of other activities to grow your business as it stands now. But you need not stop there. By using your book as the base, you can develop several products and services to expand your business even further. I'll begin with a comprehensive list to get ideas flowing. Then, I'll provide details on some of the easiest ways to get started with an information marketing business.

ELEVEN OPPORTUNITIES TO LEVERAGE
YOUR BOOK INTO NEW INCOME

1. Licensing and Area-Exclusive Businesses

With licensing, you give other businesses or persons the right to use your content. It may be for a specific period of time, within a certain geographic area, or both. You can license your book, as I described in an earlier chapter, with the example of Dr. Charles Martin. You can also license an information product based on your book, or a system such as a coaching program. Most licenses are area-exclusive, meaning that entrepreneurs buy the rights to operate a business using your proprietary content within a specific geographic location.

2. Teleseminars and Webinars

If you spend any time on the Internet, you've likely participated in, or at least had the opportunity to take part in, a teleseminar or webinar. Information marketers offer them regularly, charging anywhere from $19 to $39 per call. They also use teleseminars and webinars as a value-added feature for membership or coaching programs. And many business owners offer free teleseminars or webinars to attract new customers and leads. Chapters in your book provide the perfect content for any of these teleseminar or webinar scenarios.

3. Consulting and Coaching

A book contributes to your coaching and consulting business in two ways. First, it outlines your core beliefs, philosophies, and strategies. Second, people who resonate with these philosophies often become your coaching or consulting clients. So in this sense, your book is an important method of transforming people from those who are interested in your message to those who become your clients.

4. Memberships and Associations

If your readers and fans want higher-value information from you on a regular basis, you have the perfect opportunity to form an association or other form of membership. Members receive perks such as monthly teleseminars or webinars, newsletters, forums, information-exchange opportunities, and more. In exchange, you gain the benefit of regular monthly income. Robert Skrob is the expert in creating associations, having done it for numerous information marketers. Check the Resources section at the back of the book for Robert's contact information.

5. Done-for-You Businesses

When you provide how-to advice in your book, some readers will follow it. However, others want someone else to do it for them. If you can bundle your product or service into a complete, turnkey system for clients, a "done-for-you" business may be an ideal strategy. For example, if you offer marketing, you can include a done-for-you, pay per click ad service. A tax accountant could provide money management services for entrepreneurs. And a writer might prepare done-for-you newsletters that customers can send to clients. With a little imagination, you can tap into the done-for-you rage and provide services for an increasing number of busy people who are ready to hand their tasks to others.

6. Continuity Programs

Continuity programs can apply to almost any of the services or products on this list. It may be a monthly membership, a regular done-for-you service, or a product shipped to customers every month. If you can apply a continuity program to your business, you create a steady and predictable cash flow.

7. Physical Products

Many entrepreneurs use their books to create information marketing products ranging from audio books and DVDs to home study kits. Your book provides perfect, ready-to-go content that can easily be repurposed and reused for these products. There is tremendous opportunity here, which I'll talk about more below.

8. Private Label Opportunities

While similar to licensing, there are distinct differences. When people pay you for a "private label," they use your book or business but label it as their own. Depending on how you structure the deal, you can also receive royalties.

9. Speaking

Many authors will say that speaking and writing a book go hand in hand. As an author, your book naturally positions you as a speaker and this is a great way to make extra money.

10. Software and Apps

I'll be honest in saying that only a few authors can develop a web-based software application or an app based on principles in their book. However, if you are one of the few, this opportunity is golden. And keep in mind you don't need to be a programming whiz to do it. You can choose from plenty of talented software developers to create your application.

11. Seminars and Events

This is one of the more sophisticated ways to use your book. If you have developed a true fan base, you should hold events. It's a perfect opportunity to foster rapport with the people who provide the highest value to your company. You can also position a book to drive people to a special seminar, at which you can build relationships with long-term, high-value customers.

I've included a lot on this list, and it's only an overview of the opportunities available to you. So at this point, you may be wondering where to start. This next list provides some of the easiest and fastest ways that most authors can leverage books into money-making opportunities.

AUDIO BOOKS AND RECORDED SPEECHES OR SEMINARS

When it comes to creating products, one of the easiest to produce is an audio book. For many people, listening to a recording may be the only way they will digest your content. An audio book gives them the choice to listen when they have time, such as during a long, boring commute to work. Offering your book in audio format allows you to capture prospects who may never read it otherwise. And keep in mind, some people want to read your book, and then listen to it as well, or vice-versa. An audio book gives them this option.

However, turning your book into an audio format is not as simple as reading into a tape recorder. You have a choice of hiring a studio to do it, or you can do it yourself. There are advantages and disadvantages to each option.

Some authors do record their own books. However, to do this you need a high quality headset and microphone, as well as recording and editing software. You will also need to decide if you want to make the recording, or hire a professional voice artist. The advantage of doing it yourself is the opportunity to inject your personality and create a connection with your listeners. On the other hand, some voices just don't record well. In addition, you have to dedicate time to recording and editing. Where you save on out-of-pocket costs by making your own recording, you lose in time. This can be very expensive if you need to look after other money-making activities in your business.

However, the greatest disadvantage in making your own audio book is the lower sound quality. Recording with a studio is definitely more expensive, but your book will have the professional edge that many buyers expect. After recording, an audio producer will listen and remove breath, pop, click, and spit noises. If you want, they can add music or other sound effects throughout. They will then produce your recording using high-end technology that suits both CDs and MP3s.

When it comes to choosing a professional or homemade recording, consider your audience. If you want to attract professionals, your recording should be top-notch. You should also consider a professional recording if you have a complex topic or an older audience where clarity is essential. Finally, consider the time involved. If you can make money by spending time on other projects, hire a sound studio. If you publish with Advantage Media Group, we can provide this service for you.

If you regularly give speeches or seminars on your book topic, you can also produce live CD or DVD recordings of these events. People are generally more forgiving when it comes to sound quality for a recorded live event or interview. I still suggest that you use a professional since it takes specialized equipment to get a decent quality recording at a live event.

You have different options when it comes to using your audio and video recordings. For example, you can sell your audio book, CDs, or DVDs individually. A DVD or CD can be bundled with your book at a special price or offered as a premium for another product, such as membership. Finally, you can include one or more in a home-study kit, which I'll talk about more in a moment.

E-Books

You should also offer your book in Kindle, iPad, and Nook formats. Since many people read their books this way now, you want to provide your audience with these options. Compared to creating an audio book, this is relatively easy to do in four steps:

1. Format your book using Microsoft Word or similar software

2. Turn your Word document into a .prc document using software you can download from the Internet

3. Preview your book using Kindle Previewer

4. Register your book with Amazon

You can do all of the above on your own, using Word and other software, or you can start right on Amazon's website and use its software. Of course, the other alternative is to hire someone to do it for you. Once again, you need to determine where using your time provides the greatest value. Authors who publish with Advantage automatically get their book in Kindle, iPad and Nook formats.

How-To Kits or Courses

You have a wide range of options with instructive kits or courses. Some authors have created home-study kits that sell for 20–50 times the price of their book. A home-study kit could include some or all of the following:

- audio CDs

- DVDs

- workbooks

- example templates, forms, or other items

- access to special teleseminars or websites

- recorded seminars, round-table discussions, or consultations

Thanks to the Internet, you can also offer self-paced, online courses, or even create your own online university.

> If you want to turn your content into an online course and tap into an incredible, passive revenue stream, request a free copy of my new book, *Log on and Learn: How to Quickly and Easily Create Online Courses that Expand your Brand, Cultivate Customers, and Make You Money While You Sleep.* Visit **LogOnAndLearnBook.com/BTB** today!

Continuity Programs

After attracting new leads and customers through their books, entrepreneurial authors often provide one or more continuity programs. This is important because continuity programs add regular, ongoing income to your company, something that any business would benefit from. Plus, you have several possibilities to choose from, some of which are relatively easy to implement.

One of the most common is a monthly membership program. This usually includes access to a special website and/or resource directories, e-mail messages from the author, regular teleseminars, and a newsletter, preferably a mailed hard copy.

If you're a member of the Glazer-Kennedy Insider's Circle, or GKIC, these methods should be familiar to you. You will also recognize the GKIC Ladder of Success. After starting at the Gold Level, members can ascend to Gold Luxury, Diamond Luxury, Platinum Info-Mastermind, and finally, Titanium Info-Mastermind. Membership perks and prices rise as you climb the ladder.

Most people will begin the climb on your ladder after reading your book. Many will choose the first level of membership to start, although some skip this and go right to the top. However, most will climb your ladder, rung by rung, advancing from general membership to a group-coaching program, and finally, one-on-one coaching or mastermind groups.

Memberships can, and often do, continue for years, while coaching programs tend to be for a set period, such as 12 months. When one coaching group finishes, you should have new participants waiting in the wings and ready to go. Your goal should be to attract newcomers through your book, then into your membership program, and finally, up the ladder, just as GKIC does.

Done-for-you services are another way to create ongoing income. At Advantage Media Group, we have a done-for-you marketing, branding, and positioning program called Book the Business™. We provide marketing services for authors who want to market their books but have little time to do it. While this is a comprehensive program, you can begin with something simple.

One of the benefits of continuity programs is they range from simple to very complex. Of course, your monthly income rises with complexity, but you can easily start with the simple versions. Get monthly income flowing in, and then build from there.

How These Entrepreneurs Created Multiple Revenue Streams with Their Books

So far, I've provided you with information and strategies to create new income with your book. Now, I'd like to give you some examples of business owners who put these strategies to work for their business.

Steve Clark, New School Selling

Steve Clark (**newschoolselling.com**) is a sales coach and consultant who transformed his business after writing his book *Profitable Persuasion*. He started by creating podcasts based on the book's chapters. Today, he has several information products including an audio book, CDs, DVD sets, and a soon-to-be released training kit, *Renegade Selling Strategies for the New Economy*.

I'd like to note an interesting tactic that Steve uses to repurpose older content. New visitors to his website can get a free, six-CD set as well as a sales skills analysis kit just by providing contact information. Steve has given new life to older products by using them as lead generation tools. It is also a great strategy for building a list.

Steve also offers a monthly membership program called the *Inner Circle*. Modeled after the very successful GKIC Gold Level program, members receive monthly newsletters, audio CDs, live coaching calls, and access to a members-only website. Steve also provides additional training information and articles for members to review at their leisure. Not surprisingly, chapters from his book form the basis for his eight-week *Jump Start TeleClass Training Program*, which is another member benefit.

Steve has taken the next step in continuity programs by offering limited territories for New School Certified Business Consultants. He provides entrepreneurs with a "proven turnkey business model" in return for licensing fees. Since he already had a system to teach people, developing a model for others to follow and execute was a logical next step. This also adds another income stream to his business.

Ron Seaver, "Brought to You By ...", the Ultimate Sponsorship Sales System

After spending 25 years connecting corporate sponsors with sports organizations and individual athletes, Ron Seaver (**sponsorshipsystem.com**) decided to use this experience to develop a new business. He wrote the book "that started it all," *Getting Yourself Sponsored—For Authors, Associations or Any Business... Your Blueprint to Unlock Brand New Revenue Streams*. However, this was just his first step.

Ron went on to develop the "Brought to You By..." System. This home-study kit includes:

- Three manuals and accompanying CDs, all of which expand on content from the book

- A Fast Start CD

- Three bonus manuals: *Where Do I Start?, Let's Talk About Money, A Case of Gold*

- Fill-in-the-blank templates

- Certificate for a free written evaluation from Ron

- A copy of a recent National Sports Forum Corporate & Industry Survey, along with a "special" DVD presentation on the survey, in which leading sponsors indicate what they are looking for when choosing which people, places, and events to sponsor

Let's explore what Ron included in his system. The material for the three manuals all comes from Ron's book. He simply expanded on the content and provided more examples. The CDs provide an additional way for his customers to learn and understand his concepts. What's great about this is once he had his book, creating this course material was relatively easy.

The templates are systems that Ron has used throughout his career, so they were easy and inexpensive to add. The free evaluation is another no-cost addition as well as the survey, which he had on hand anyway. This survey outlines reasons why corporations will sponsor an individual or association, so it's easy to see why someone interested in sponsorships would find it valuable. All of these bonus items provide real value for Ron's customers, yet they cost virtually nothing to include in the kit.

Finally, three bonus manuals provide additional information that Ron prepared for this course. However, he can repurpose and reuse this content elsewhere, whether in a live seminar, on a bonus CD, or in a blog post. Thus, his time to prepare these manuals will go a lot further for his business. And his customers are happy with bonus items that are relatively easy and inexpensive to provide.

I've dissected Ron's course because I want to make an important point. Once Ron had his book, developing a course was a logical next step. How-to books such as Ron's are relatively easy to expand into a home-study kit, an online course, or both. And consider this: the "Brought to You By..." System sells for $2,497. That is a lot more than one book, which Ron sells for $19.99. In addition, the kit is another step to move people up his product ladder.

The next step on Ron's ladder is continuity programs. At the first level, he provides affordable monthly coaching calls. Every month, members get the latest trends and tips on sponsorship from Ron while having a chance to ask questions. Ron also provides a link to a private website where members can download MP3 files so they can listen to past calls at any time.

For customers who want more, Ron offers the Platinum Sponsorship Group. Members enjoy platinum group calls, individual calls, a private coaching day with Ron, and two platinum retreats for an annual fee of $13,000. Now, it's pretty easy to do the math here. Even with just half a dozen members, Ron has added a comfortable income cushion to his business.

Finally, Ron's annual Sponsorship Bootcamp provides every customer with an opportunity to learn with Ron while meeting and interacting with others. Ron offers his bootcamp at three different price levels:

- First-time attendees who have already purchased the "Brought to You By…" System

- First-time attendees with the "Brought to You By…" System included in the price of the bootcamp

- Sponsorship Bootcamp "returners"

By offering three different price levels, Ron fills more seats, especially with the half-price rate for bootcamp alumni. By encouraging past attendees to return, Ron creates an event that people look forward to every year. This is one way to make an event sustainable.

It's interesting to note that Ron continues to offer his book at a relatively low cost on his website. By providing easily accessible copies of his book, Ron gets people interested and engaged. His book builds rapport and demonstrates the value he provides. He then moves prospects up his ladder to higher-priced items.

By following this system, Ron has built a lucrative information marketing business. Once developed, many of his products require little time and input from him. His "Brought to You By …" System rolls in the money with virtually no additional effort. Plus, it keeps customers coming back for more, higher-ticket services.

Tom Antion, Public Speaking and Internet Marketing

Tom Antion (**tomantion.com**) began his information marketing business with his book, *Wake 'Em Up Business Presentations*. As the title implies, Tom provides tips and strategies for anyone to be a better speaker. Tom took a route similar to Ron Seaver's with a bit of a twist. He began by developing the different chapters of his book into individual CDs and CD sets that he sells on his website at prices ranging from $29.95 to $197.

In addition to the CDs, Tom offers DVDs, e-books, and video e-courses at different price levels to match the desires of his varied buyers. However, Tom went a step further. He combined his book with additional information to create the *Wake 'Em Up Speakers System* that includes:

- six DVDs

- fast-track action guide

- his book

- five valuable bonuses

Tom combined additional information with his book to create the system. For example, on the DVDs, he features clips of himself—and other well-known speakers—in which he points out what to do as well as what *not* to do. Today, he sells the system for $997, or $1,597 with a payment plan. Not bad when you consider he started with a book that sells for $24.95.

Tom also provides higher-end services for interested customers including a consulting and a mentoring program. He has even founded an online Internet marketing school. However, the one lesson I hope you take away from Tom's experience is this: if you're not sure where to begin, start small as Tom did. Start with an audio book, or CDs on one or more chapters of your book, or both. Your experience in developing these products will make your next steps easier, and your income will grow as you go along.

Robert Skrob, Information Marketing Association

The Information Marketing Association (**info-marketing.org**) is affiliated with GKIC and provides resources for people who want to build an information marketing business. When president, Robert Skrob had the idea for the association, one of the first things he did was write the book *The Official Get Rich Guide to Information Marketing: Build a Million Dollar Business Within 12 Months*. A valuable resource in itself, the book also acts as a gateway to membership in the association.

Business owners from countless industries and backgrounds pay a monthly fee for benefits that include a newsletter, teleconferences, online networking, free content to use in their own newsletters or websites, and more. Keep in mind, the association is an additional business for Robert. He keeps busy with his company, Membership Services, Inc., along with the coaching and consulting services he provides. His book and the IMA are one of Robert's many ongoing revenue streams.

Bo Burlingham, Small Giant Communities

Mention the name, Bo Burlingham, and many in the business community will recognize him as an author, consultant, speaker, and Inc.'s editor at large. In 2006 he released his second book, *Small Giants: Companies that Choose to be Great Instead of Big*. He based his book on the idea that small and inspiring companies share six common characteristics, which he dubbed "business mojo."

Bo probably had little idea that his book would create what some would call a cult following. However, small business owners gravitated to his message. Many choose to be great rather than big and they want to share this value openly with others. So in 2009, Bo founded the Small Giants Community (**smallgiants.org**). Members pay $500 annually for training programs, educational materials, conferences, and the right to be known as an "individual in pursuit of business mojo."

Today, Small Giants is an international organization with a growing staff. In addition to its regular services, it offers training programs that members can attend at a discount. Small Giants is now a worldwide phenomenon that started with one book.

All of these entrepreneurs created new businesses or expanded existing ones by leveraging their books. They now have income where none existed before. This is something any business owner would be happy to have, myself included. Yet sometimes just by having a book, new revenue opportunities will find you, and they often come from unexpected sources.

Money Does Grow on Trees; the Serendipity Created by Books

When you write a book, you declare your business philosophies and solutions to specific problems. You create a bridge to people who share your beliefs or need your answers. And some of these people will view you as an ally or potential business partner. This is when the unexpected happens.

And this is exactly what happened to Steve Sax. I mentioned in an earlier chapter that Steve is a retired baseball player who now has a coaching and speaking business aimed at professionals and companies. However, after reading his book, some organizations have hired Steve to run baseball clinics. This is something he never thought of when developing his business model. However, the clinics are a fun way to drive additional revenue into his business.

After retiring from professional golf, Rick Sessinghaus began coaching executives in their golf games. To kick-start his business, he published *Golf: The Ultimate Mind Game*. The operators of select golf facilities and franchises located across the country took notice. As a result, he now speaks at some of their sites every month, and his book was "the initial door opener."

Jennifer Nicole Lee has also experienced this phenomenon. Jennifer is a fitness model, information-marketing business owner, and author of four books, with another in the works. In one of her books, she endorsed Endermologie, which is equipment for tightening skin and reducing cellulite. Well, it happened that an intern working at Daniele Henkel in Canada read her book. This would mean little if it weren't for the fact that this company is the worldwide distributor of Endermologie. After the intern shared the book with the company's CEO, they asked Jennifer to be their US ambassador.

They also recently collaborated with her to open the new JNL Beauty and Wellness center in Coral Gables, Florida.

After working with hundreds of authors, I have countless stories like these. You never know who may read your book one day. By getting your book out there, executing your marketing plan, and creating new business opportunities, anything can happen.

TWELVE

HOW TO USE YOUR BOOK TO GET OTHERS TO PAY FOR YOUR MARKETING

By Adam Witty

ould you be interested in reaching new audiences, building your list, and growing sales with little increase to your marketing budget? Can you imagine another business helping you with your marketing, or even paying you to do it?

I think most would agree the chance of this happening in business-as-usual conditions is virtually zero. But this is where a book changes the game.

Your book is a powerful marketing tool. When businesses have audiences who could benefit from the information in it, they will gladly promote it for you. They gain by keeping their customers happy with new, interesting, and helpful information, while you collect new leads and customers.

With a book, it is easy to create these win-win situations. The reason for this is simple. People truly value books because they go beyond entertainment. They make us stronger, wiser, wealthier, and more. This is why so many are happy to buy a book, and even happier to get one as a gift.

So, the first thing to do is to ask this question: "Who would benefit by making their audience aware of the information I have to share?" Then, filter this question through each of these 10 opportunities to build a list of potential partners:

1. Your Vendors

Where did you spend money last year? Some of these businesses may be marketing to the same potential customers as you. If they aren't in direct competition, this is a golden opportunity to develop your own version of "co-op advertising."

Your vendor can offer your book as a premium giveaway in her ads, whether online, in print, on radio, or on TV. She will have an incentive to get people into her stores or onto her website, and you will have increased exposure without paying for the additional advertising.

I provide this advice with two additional recommendations. First, expect your vendors to help. You are their customer. It should be important to them to keep you happy. Plus, they have a vested interest in ensuring your success. The greater your success, the more business they can expect from you. Second, make sure your ad copy is top-notch.

2. Clients and Customers

Next, comb through your list. Like vendors, you may have clients/customers who will promote your book to their audience. You may also have clients who are happy to share your book simply because they are your true fans. Do whatever you can to make it easy for them to do so.

There are different ways you can facilitate giveaways. One of the easiest is to simply give your client free copies of your book. If you have mentioned your client in your book, you can go a step further. Give your client a "congratulatory" letter that he can include when sharing your book. The letter essentially provides your client with an opportunity to say, "I'm featured in this book and I'd like you to have a complimentary copy."

If your client has a large customer list, consider a special edition, printed just for that client. This edition can include an introduction written by your client, or an additional chapter that tells your client's story. If you're wondering about the cost of doing this, these two criteria can help you decide if it is worthwhile:

1. You know how much a customer is worth to your business and your client's list is a golden source, and

2. You know how much you are willing to pay to obtain a customer.

For example, if you project two new customers because of this exercise and each customer is worth $5,000 annually, you can spend up to $9,999. This, by the way, is a quick and easy way to determine the maximum you should spend for any lead generating activity.

Finally, consider any client who has retail outlets, online or off. If they sell to people you want as customers, ask them to give your book away as a premium. Their customers get an unexpected bonus, and you reach a new, targeted market.

3. Complementary Businesses

After reviewing your vendor and client lists, move on to businesses that complement yours. This includes any business with products or services that add value for your customers, just as your business provides value for theirs. You may recall the example of a commercial real-estate broker and an office furniture store from an earlier chapter. This is one of countless possibilities.

A tax lawyer complements an accountant who concentrates on corporate taxes. Financial planners could work with attorneys specializing in estate planning. A cosmetic surgeon's counterpart could be a specialist in cosmetic dentistry.

If you're a lawyer focusing on elder law, you could partner with assisted living centers or retirement homes. These homes could use your book as bait, giving it to anyone who comes for a tour. Getting your book in the hands of your grade-A prospects is better than selling a few copies at Barnes & Noble any day.

An actual example is Advantage Media Group and GKIC. Advantage is the publisher for professionals. So, we target professionals of all types including entrepreneurs and small-business owners. GKIC markets to nearly the same audience. However, they offer something completely different: how-to business building and marketing advice. Advantage and GKIC provide complementary services to the same customer. Therefore, it makes sense for both companies to share some of our marketing. By doing so, we both save money and create opportunities to grow our customer base. Keep your eyes open for similar opportunities in your business.

Finally, earlier in this book, I mentioned Brian Fricke and his book *Worry Free Retirement*. You may recall he is a financial advisor who uses his book as a lead generator for his business.

One day, out of the blue, Brian got a call from a marketing agency that specializes in promoting senior retirement communities. They had found his book on the Internet, thanks, in part, to its title. The agency hired Brian to speak at an event designed to attract potential buyers and tenants. While they used Brian as their lead generator, he was able to market his business to his golden audience.

This story could have ended here with Brian earning some extra income and going back to business as usual. However, this event opened Brian's eyes to new business opportunities. He is now sending marketing materials to agencies that cater to retirement community developers across the country. And he is considering other industries that market to the same client he does. His plan is to find companies who will hire him to speak and give his book to their customers. In essence, they will pay Brian to do his own lead generation.

4. Associations

Don't forget associations in your market, especially those where you are a member. Small Giants, for example, lists books authored by members on its website. If you belong to similar organizations, you may be able to do the same. If not, ask if you can give your book to fellow members as a membership benefit. Another alternative is to give your book to members during meetings or other events. Another option is your local chamber of commerce. You can often speak, set up a display, and give away your book at a wide variety of events or meetings. As a member, you piggyback on the chamber's events to promote your book.

5. Events

When it comes to events, you have two ways to create win-win scenarios. Option number one is to find all conferences in your market that cater to people you want to reach. Then, look for events at which your service or products can provide added value for attendees.

Event organizers are always looking for ways to give their audiences more. One way they do this is by providing a great "goodies" bag. If you attend conferences, you likely have a collection. It's the tote bag you get at registration filled with pens, pads, magazines, and so on. Why not get your book in there too? If your book complements event topics, many organizers will be happy to provide each registrant with a copy. And you get your book in the hands of targeted prospects.

Your second option is to arrange your own event in a place that adds exclusivity and appeal. I'm not suggesting a large, expensive, difficult-to-organize conference. I am talking about an evening with the author in your local bookstore. Many Barnes & Noble stores have areas or even rooms for author meet-and-greets. Independent bookstores routinely use the coffee shop next door for author readings.

There are numerous benefits in holding an event like this. An evening with the author in itself sounds exclusive. Presenting it in a coffee shop or a bookstore enhances the appeal. It's less formal and more comfortable for many people. And many authors find they attract a crowd by offering a free copy of their book. The bookstores and coffee shops are happy to cater to customers. You attract potential customers who may have never walked into the more sales-like environment of your office. Plus, it's relatively easy to organize with the bookstore, and they will help with promoting the event.

6. Trade Shows

If you've ever walked the aisles of a trade show, you've seen them: calendars, pens, candy, tote bags, or whatever creative giveaways companies might dream up. I've been to shows where people have literally stormed a booth just to grab a popular goody before it's gone. Keep in mind most companies don't want this to happen, or at least they shouldn't. The idea is to attract prospects to talk with you, not to grab a freebie and run.

This is where your book provides a significant benefit for companies that complement your business. If your message provides value for their customers and prospects, they can give your book away instead of the same-old, boring pen. If you sell your book at a wholesale rate, it makes it easier for them to justify the cost. Plus, they now have a giveaway with heft. They can provide a free copy of your book in exchange for contact information. While most people won't part with their e-mail address for a pen, they certainly will for a book that interests them.

If you're attending the conference as well, why not offer to do a book signing at the booth? The company can promote an hour with the author, which will attract new people to the booth in addition to bringing back others who visited earlier. Once again, the benefits are obvious. The company attracts prospects to its booth while providing a free distribution outlet for you and your content.

7. Teleseminars and Webinars

This is one of my favorites because you can do teleseminars and webinars from the comfort of your home or office at any time you choose. Dan does this brilliantly. Before launching a new book, Dan has a list of affiliates, joint-venture partners, and complementary businesses ready to go. He schedules teleseminars with any that have an audience who would be interested in his book, in his services, or both.

Chris Hurn also uses teleseminars to full advantage. He recently told me that one of his calls included a martial arts guru and his audience. You might wonder, at first, why an expert in small business loans would be interested in talking with people in the martial arts industry. However, for Chris, it makes perfect sense. He has financed a number of martial arts studios over the years, probably more than any other lender. By getting studio owners to read his book, visit his Facebook page, or monitor his blog, they get to know him. When the time comes for them to purchase commercial property, he will be the first lender they look to for help.

A book provides your host with two significant advantages. For one, it gives him something fresh and relevant to promote to his audience. A new topic gives people a reason to tune in. Second, you can offer a free or low-cost copy to all those who provide you with their contact information. If promoted well, this will attract more people to your host's teleseminar. Your host provides his audience with an educational topic and a valuable gift while you add more leads to your marketing funnel.

8. Speaking Opportunities

If you could get a room full of potential customers, would you like an opportunity to talk with them, even for just a few minutes? Your book can make this happen. From large events to small workshops, your book provides access to top prospects.

Here's a story from my own business. It begins in Chicago, with marketing consultant Steve Sipress. Every month, Steve holds a meeting at which members learn about direct marketing and getting the most out of their businesses. His group includes entrepreneurs, professionals, and business owners, all of whom are top prospects for my business.

Now, Steve and I know one another, thanks to our meeting through mutual friends. He gave me a standing invitation to speak to his group whenever I was in the Chicago area. Well, the day finally arrived when I had to travel to Chicago for business. So, I arranged with Steve to spend an hour with his members.

That evening, Steve introduced me as the author of *21 Ways to Build Your Business with a Book*. I spoke for an hour, outlining the top 10 benefits of being an author and using your book to generate new business. This was relatively easy to do since the content for my presentation came directly from my book. At the end, I offered our Fast Start Author Program™, which provides a complete book strategy and outline for writing and publishing a book, **advantagefamily.com/FSAP**.

After finishing, I gave everyone a complimentary copy of my book. And here's where it gets interesting. At least 30 people asked me to autograph their copy. Even more surprising, 15 or so asked if they could have their picture taken with me. Now, I am not a celebrity by any means. I can certainly walk the streets without being recognized or having paparazzi chasing me. But just for that night, this audience viewed me as someone special, an expert who provided them with useful information.

This situation was a win-win-win for everyone. Steve won because he provided members with something different as well as valuable information. His members won by learning about a new opportunity to grow their business. I won with several new customers signing up for the Fast Start Author Program.

Although everyone benefitted, I still feel I came out ahead. The cost to acquire these customers was a few hours of my time to attend the meeting along with 70 copies of my book. Steve did all the work to get people to the event, as well as paying for food and beverages. I only had to show up, yet everyone was happy to have me there. What could be better than that when it comes to marketing your business?

This works for any business, whether at local meetings or national conferences. Not surprisingly, I recommend starting locally. A host of organizations such as local business improvement associations and service clubs are always looking for new presenters with interesting information. Pick those with audiences that include your potential customers. After speaking, offer an entry-level service or product that will draw people into your business. Use your book as bait or a premium. I know of several authors who do this with great success.

If you're not comfortable with speaking, why not offer to sponsor coffee for the evening? In return, the host can introduce you to the audience. You can set up a display, provide everyone with books in exchange for contact information, and chat one-on-one with members over coffee. You may be surprised at how quickly you grow comfortable with being in front of an audience, and ultimately, speaking. Plus, this is a great way to grow your list and your customer base.

9. Newsletters

Most business owners will jump at a chance to expand their list, or if starting from ground-zero, to develop one. A book provides you with an exceptional opportunity to do this through newsletters, whether your own or those of complementary businesses.

If you publish and mail a newsletter to your list, use excerpts from your book as articles. This is an easy way to generate content, as well as interest in your book. Offer your readers a free copy. After all, if they are interested in your newsletter, they are interested in you and your message. Why not give them more? Another tactic is to offer your book as a premium for an entry-level product or service. This can encourage people on your list to take the next step and become a client/customer. In both cases, you gain by adding value for your prospects without adding expense to your newsletter budget.

Newsletters of complementary companies provide excellent opportunities to expand and develop your list as well. Start by writing an article based on one top idea from your book. Or, go a step further and prepare a series of articles. At the bottom of every article, provide a 30-second elevator pitch for your business, as well as an offer that drives people to your website to get a free copy of your book. Create urgency by adding a time limit, or limiting the number of books available.

Then, review your list of complementary businesses. Find businesses that send newsletters to your target audience. Let them know you have articles they can use. You can sweeten this request by offering to include their article in your newsletter. If you don't have a newsletter, suggest another benefit, such as including their ad on your website or adding their display in your store.

Once again, everybody wins. Your article provides easy content for your newsletter partner. If you reciprocate by putting their article in your newsletter, they reach more prospective customers. Subscribers gain by having a new source of information. And you win with the opportunity to build a list that you can nurture, with little added cost to your bottom line.

10. Internet TV

I mentioned Internet TV in an earlier chapter, and I'm bringing it up again because you can get companies to help you pay for this powerful marketing medium. Let's look at the example of Andrew Lock, the "maverick marketer" for small business and entrepreneurs. In early 2008 Andrew aired his first episode of *Help, My Business Sucks!*, an Internet TV show filled with tips to market small businesses. Today, after 165 shows, he has more than 100,000 viewers.

Of course, he now uses his show to market his information products and membership programs to a large audience. This alone would be music to the ears of any entrepreneur. However, Andrew also earns money with every broadcast he does. If you watch a show, you will see that he announces a sponsor at the start of every episode. He also features products of the experts he interviews. It's a safe bet that he gets a portion of revenues from any sales they make by appearing on his show.

Almost any business owner or entrepreneur can do this, or something similar. For example, if you're nervous about diving into an Internet TV show, why not start with webinars? To start, you can feature chapters from your book as your webinar topics. This makes it easy to develop your content. Then, look for sponsors who want to reach your audience. They get a better bang for their advertising buck, while you get revenue that pays for your marketing.

Bonus Tip: This Little-Known Way to Market Your Book is Free

Whether selling to a local or national market, you want to make sure your book is easy to find. People must be able to locate your book in more places than just your website. This includes everything from Amazon to independent, local bookstores.

However, for anyone who sells to local or regional markets, this next tip is especially important. Get your book into local libraries. Again, the focus is not on selling your book. It is on getting new customers. Some people may hear you on the radio or see you on the local morning show. They won't buy your book, but they *will* borrow it. Dan has anecdotal stories of practices acquiring $50,000 patients this way. It's easy. It's essentially free. And it can be very effective.

Think for a moment on the power of multiplicity and leverage. The strategies I have provided bring these forces to your marketing, and your book is at the heart of it all. Instead of talking with people, one by one, you can literally reach hundreds, even thousands, with little to no added cost. A book leverages the strengths of people, processes, media, and economies of scale to deliver more customers for your marketing dollar.

FAST ACTION
IMPLEMENTATION, RESOURCES, AND THE
ONE SECRET
NOBODY TELLS YOU

THIRTEEN

PUTTING YOUR PLAN INTO ACTION

By Adam Witty

BEFORE YOU WRITE: SEVEN STEPS TO CREATING A MONEY-MAKING BOOK

book is your business game changer. Dan and I can name hundreds of authors, including ourselves, who have transformed their business with a book. The sampling of success stories below illustrates the extensive possibilities that business owners have as authors:

- an extra $1,000 in income at every speaking engagement, simply by selling books and spin-off items at the back of the room

- fees for one keynote speech net $15,000

- a new contract worth more than $45,000

- a 3 to 1 return on the book investment from free publicity alone

- a position as spokesperson for a nationally advertised fitness product

- regular appearances on national news programs

- a 40 percent increase in the customer base

- additional income of $1 million by selling information products based on a book

- speaking fees increased by 30 to 50 percent

- a 30 percent increase in patient load just 18 months after publishing

- bookings for speaking engagements doubling in one year

These results come from people in a range of professions: a chiropractor, fitness model, financial advisor, lawyer, business consultant, professional speaker, and more. Each has unique goals for his or her business. Their books span a range of topics. And everyone has distinct marketing objectives. Yet in spite of these differences, all took the same three steps to achieve their success:

- They defined a strategy for their book

- They created a marketing plan, and

- They implemented it

It all seems so simple, yet many authors miss one or more of these steps when it comes to their book. However, it's no different than developing a strategy for a new website or a marketing plan for your business. A solid business strategy for your book is the secret to making real money as an author.

So, where do you begin? I suggest starting with the steps below. Even if you already have a book on shelves, some of these steps will still help in bringing attention to your business. You'll note that each step contains at least one question. I believe asking questions is the best way to develop a plan. When it comes to a book, the possibilities to promote and grow your business are endless. Asking the right questions will help you develop strategies that work best for you.

1. Determine the Purpose of Your Book

Although this seems basic, this is your most important step. You need to consider how a book can help you achieve your strategic business goals. After working with hundreds of authors, I've noticed that most have two over-arching business goals they want a book to fulfill. Number one is generating new leads. Number two is launching a new business.

I've provided two questions below, along with examples from other authors, to help you determine your book's purpose. After exploring both questions, it will be easier to engineer a book that achieves your business goals.

Who are you writing to? What doors do you need to open?

A book is a conduit to reaching certain segments of your market. Dan is a master at designing books for this purpose. He could have written one book on marketing and been done with the subject. However, he has created ongoing discussion and interest by writing additional books tailored to certain marketing themes. For example, *Marketing to the Affluent* places marketing in a completely new context. It's the same for *Marketing to Boomers and*

Seniors. By narrowing his main topic, he reaches new audiences—and new customers.

This is just as important for small business owners or professionals, perhaps even more so. By focusing attention on a segment of your market, you appeal more to that audience. Your business stands out.

So start by asking yourself, "To whom am I writing? Whom do I want to attract to my business?" By doing this, you can position your book to not only stand out in a specific market but also to attract your ideal client/customer.

For example, I mentioned Travis Miller and Jimmy Vee in an earlier chapter. Their book *Invasion of the Profit Snatchers: A Practical Guide to Increasing Sales Without Cutting Prices & Protecting Your Dealership from Looters, Moochers & Vendors Gone Wild* is clearly aimed at auto dealers. Through this book, they have developed a very profitable business, Rich Dealers. Yet they began as broad-based marketing experts. By focusing on a certain group within their market, this book has created an entirely new business for them.

Dentist and author Dr. Charles Martin knows how to stand out in a crowded field. He wrote *This Won't Hurt a Bit: A Consumer's Guide to Dentistry* to differentiate his practice from the competition. It worked, but he didn't stop there. His second book, *Don't Sugar Coat It: The Story of Diabetes and Dentistry—What They Didn't Tell You* appealed to a new segment of his market. Think of it this way: if you have diabetes, you may have missed the first book, but this title will definitely catch your attention.

We've mentioned several times how the title of "author" provides nearly instant credibility. Your book makes you a go-to expert in your field. This alone shines the spotlight on you.

However, you can narrow your topic even further. By demonstrating expertise in a specific area, you can elevate yourself even further above a crowd.

This is what John Dolan did with his book *Negotiate like the Pros*. As a criminal defense lawyer, he could have written about a wide range of topics on the law. However, John chose a specific topic because he wanted positioning as an expert in one arena. His plan worked. In addition to his law practice, John has an active speaking business. He speaks to groups ranging from lawyers to sales staff at Apple, or scouts for the Texas Rangers. It's a wide variety of audiences, but all pay top dollar to learn better negotiation techniques. His book laid the pathway to reach different segments of a broad market.

As an added bonus, John leveraged his book to create another business. He offers classes on negotiation skills for lawyers who need to fulfill required continuing education hours. Again, his book provides him with the expert status required to teach such courses. This wasn't a happenstance occurrence. Rather, John did this by *design*.

A book can also position you in a new light if you need to switch gears in your business. Rick Sessinghaus knows this well. If you're an avid golfer, you may recognize his name. Once part of the PGA tour, the day came when Rick lost his tour card. He had plenty of skills to be a golf coach, and he knew he wanted to work with business executives. However, he had to find a way to reach them, or in a sense, to join their ranks.

Like the media, corporations respond to the expertise authorship provides. It is often the tipping point they need to hire you over another similar consultant or business. So, Rick wrote his book with the corporate audience in mind. As a result, he gained the standing and clout to open doors of CEO suites. Today, he reigns as *the* golf coach for Fortune 500 companies.

Your book will provide instant positioning as an expert. Before writing, consider whether you can advance your business, or even develop a new one, by attracting a specific audience. You can then tailor your book topic, language, and tone to achieve your business objectives.

How Can You Educate Your Audience?

In addition to determining who your audience will be, consider the information they will need. By providing helpful information, you establish a relationship with your readers. They understand who you are, what you're doing, and equally important, why you do it. Your goal is to create a bond of trust.

Education is especially important for any complex topic or field. Anyone selling highly technical products will tell you that educating prospects is the straightest path to long-term customers. Yet education benefits any profession or business.

For example, authors in medical fields often write their books, in part, to educate patients. Books allow them to answer common questions or explain procedures. They can provide advice to relieve pain, or to help readers after office hours. Many feel that patients who read their books respond better to treatment than those who don't. And, in addition to bringing new patients into their practice, they have found that their book encourages patients to stay.

Determine the information you need to include in your book. Your goal should be to build solid relationships while leaving your readers wanting more. This attracts people to you and ultimately, the additional products and services you have to offer.

2. Create Your List of Book Partners and Promoters

Once again, I have another question for you: Who are the people within your universe who want to be a part of your book? This includes people who would be interested in promoting your book to their list and/or writing a guest chapter.

When it comes to including other businesses in his books, Dan calls this "selling real estate." When designing a book, Dan creates a list of businesses and entrepreneurs who can provide relevant and useful information for his intended audience. For a certain sum, usually a preordered number of books, an interested business will get a guest chapter. For a lesser amount, he will include their story within two or three paragraphs in a regular chapter.

The featured business gains increased exposure and new marketing opportunities. Dan provides his readers with additional information, while making more money directly from the book. Dan normally doubles the amount he nets over the course of each book's lifetime by selling this "real estate."

As an alternative to selling book real estate, Dan also offers space in exchange for promotion opportunities. For example, a business may agree to buy a minimum number of copies. It may promote his book to its list, or interview Dan so he can promote it directly. Often, a business will agree to all three options.

Keep in mind, Dan doesn't tell a story solely for making money. Any material he includes must be of value to his readers. However, if he has a choice between two businesses, and one can provide access to a list of 5,000 target readers while the other can provide nothing, it's easy to see which business will get its story told.

Ideally, this should be done when constructing your outline, or at the latest, while writing your book. However, if you're well past that stage, you can still review every business you know that fits your target audience. Ask if that business will interview you in exchange for offering your book as a free premium or some other benefit. These opportunities will keep new leads flowing into your marketing pipeline.

3. Develop Your Media List

Although I've covered media extensively in a previous chapter, this question is so important, it bears repeating here. What media should you generate for your business? Develop your top-ten list of media that reaches your ideal customer. Then, when designing your book, keep this list in mind.

Let's say your list includes *Inc., Success,* and *Entrepreneur* magazines. Can you include information or a chapter in your book that appeals to their editors? Likewise, do these magazines cover topics that *your* readers would find interesting? You can include these topics in your book as well. Do they provide clues to keywords that would make your book title—and your business—easier to find by searching reporters and readers alike? By considering these questions in the early stages of your book, it will be easier to get free publicity after publishing.

4. Plan to Lead Readers Away from Your Book

When you're writing a book to advance your business, you need readers to connect with you and provide their contact information. How can you get people to go somewhere beyond your book? In other words, what can you offer them?

There are several ways to draw people away, and some are more successful than others. However, for best results, you need to:

- Include several different calls to action

- Provide more than one way to reach you, such as a phone number and tailored landing pages

- Pepper offers throughout your book, as well as on your book's cover

As for format, you can include an outright ad in a text or Johnson box. Or, you can embed offers in your text. We have used both in this book. You should do the same with yours.

The best offers provide a compelling reason for your reader to set your book down and take the extra step to find your landing page, or pick up the phone. I mentioned some of these in an earlier chapter, but the concept is so important, I am listing suggestions again, in greater detail:

- Provide an assessment or test that a reader can take to determine his strengths, weaknesses, talents, or capabilities in certain areas. Almost everyone wants to know where she lands on a comparison scale. A test to determine this is a very compelling reason to go to your website.

- Perhaps your book includes a description of a kinesiology test that determines whether someone needs a certain supplement. You can send readers to a website that provides an instructional video so they can watch and apply their own test at the same time.

- If you tell a story about someone in your book, give readers a free CD of your exclusive interview with that person.

Another alternative is to send them to your website to download a free MP3 file of the interview.

- You can provide several different tools or fill-in-the-blank templates. This might be a financial planning spreadsheet, an event-planning checklist, or thank-you-letter templates. There are countless possibilities here.

- GKIC offers a free, 60-day trial membership in all of Dan's books. You can do something similar in yours.

It's important to offer a variety of incentives, and locate them throughout your book. That way you cater to the variety of tastes and needs of your readers. The more you offer, the more you will capture.

Note also, there is a difference in making an offer to a potential customer versus a potential client. If you're trying to find new clients, such as for speaking or consulting, you want them to take a next step. However, you should consider how hard or easy you want that next step to be. Do you want to work with people of a certain income level? Do you want to coach people with specific needs? Whatever the criteria may be, many authors build some sort of screening mechanism into their offers. However, when it comes to potential customers, little or no screening is involved.

You can see this concept in action in many of Dan's books. He provides incentives to drive customers to GKIC while also fishing for clients. Potential GKIC customers can easily sign up for a free two-month membership. However, potential clients must contact Dan's office as a first step in determining if they meet his criteria.

5. Develop a Launch Strategy That Adds Value

A book launch can take several forms. If you're on any kind of list, you may have encountered some. One example is the e-mail offering several gifts from various authors or luminaries. The catch is you must purchase the newly launched book within a specified period. Over time, you will often receive several e-mails, as the authors who endorsed the first book will repeat the process for their books. It is the typical I'll-scratch-your-back-if-you-scratch-mine scenario. Of course, for it to work, authors need a large list as well as a group of complementary businesses that are willing and able to participate.

A more familiar launch is an announcement or party where authors try to generate publicity or media opportunities. In this case, the author invites everyone he or she knows, as well as media. In another format, authors may give 25 copies of their book to clients with circles of influence. In exchange, they invite these clients, and sometimes their book recipients, to an exclusive event. Still others will hold a large event or host a webinar series with attendance open to any person who buys a book.

Finally, many authors will also do whatever they can to encourage book sales so they can claim "best-seller" status. Amazon actually facilitates this by creating countless sublists that make it easy for almost anyone to have a best-selling book.

When it comes to book launches, it is easy to do what everyone else is doing. However, this is the time to ask another question: How will my launch create customers of lasting value?

The best approach is to reverse engineer your launch by looking at outcomes that will serve you best. If you need to claim "as seen on Fox News," your launch should focus on making this happen. If it's important that your book is in the hands of influencers, this should be a part of your launch strategy. The bottom line is to develop a launch that helps you achieve your business objectives—even if you're doing it differently than everyone else.

6. **Set Up a System That Drives Business to You**

Your book on its own will never amount to much. But place it within a marketing system, and you have the power to transform your business. Your system may include some or all of the following:

- book reviews and endorsements

- marketing to your list as well as those of your book partners, affiliates, and others

- distributing your book to identified people of influence including media, key people in your industry, major bloggers, clients/customers, and others

- online promotions including your website, PPC campaigns, YouTube videos, and so on

- print media such as direct mail, remnant ad space in select publications, and articles

- speaking opportunities, trade shows, or both

Just looking at this list can be overwhelming. The key is to choose the strategies that provide the best bang for *your* business. You want to use the people and media that reach your target audience. Develop your list, and stick with it. Don't try to execute your list all at once, start with the most important and work your way down.

7. Get Started!

At this point there is little additional advice I can provide, except for this: execute your plan, tweak it as needed, and keep going. Successful authors never stop. Your book is a long-term asset for your business. Remember, it really isn't about marketing your book, but rather, how you use your book to do your marketing. Incorporate your book into your marketing system, and you'll reap the rewards.

Book The Business is a marathon, not a sprint.

AFTERWORD

by Dan Kennedy

Adam Witty and his incredible team at Advantage Media Group know book publishing inside out and do a terrific job. I frequently refer my private clients to Advantage. They have a thorough, complete, efficient process. They work with both first-time and veteran authors. They dramatically shorten the time span involved. Had they existed in my first decade of business life, I could have advanced faster with less difficulty.

If you are reading this, engaged in marketing something, anything, and you do not have your own book or books and a complete strategy for profiting from them, whether with Advantage or by other means, I urge you to become a published author.

I have been prolific and relied heavily on authorship and books, so over the years I've been with the biggest publishers including Penguin and Simon & Schuster, very small houses such as Self-Counsel Press and Adams Media, mid-range publishers such as my current, principal home, Entrepreneur Press, and pay-to-publish companies such as Advantage, and, including Advantage, I've self-published books. There are different reasons, pros, cons, and difficulties with each pathway. If being unfettered and free of interference with your content matters and you are publishing primarily as a means of promoting a business, you are usually best served by a pay-to-publish house, and there is no better than Advantage.

Of course, anybody can merely print a book, just as any monkey can put letters on paper, given a typewriter. But the folks at Advantage have the expertise to guide you in good decisions every step of the way and have everything from cover design to a related website and online video production under one roof.

Regardless of how you do it, though, getting into print as the author of a well-conceived book and using it to promote yourself and your business can be a profoundly important game changer.

Last, a secret: just as the public is impressed by authors of books, would-be authors are intimidated by the prospect of writing a book. But the secret is anybody can do it. No permission from any authority needed. Fiction arguably requires talent, certainly creativity, and can be arduous. But nonfiction is comprised of what you know and what you are willing to research. *You know your "thing"*: your business, product, or service; your methods and techniques; what you do. You may take too much of it for granted because it is routine for you. But you know it. That's the only qualification required, plus a useful purpose for your book. Authors are not superior beings—but don't tell anybody.

RESOURCES & FREE
AND NEARLY FREE OFFERS

from Dan Kennedy

1. GKIC, the association of marketing-oriented entrepreneurs, business owners, professionals in private practice and sales professionals offers a comprehensive portfolio of support, including Dan's newsletters, monthly audio programs, specialized training seminars, major events, networking, coaching programs and mastermind groups. A *nearly free trial membership* is available (only shipping & handling required), which includes the No B.S. Marketing Letter, Gold Letter, *Marketing Gold* audio CD, full access to online resources, and a series of webinars. To get more information and enroll, visit **www.DanKennedy.com/bookofbusiness**

2. The Information Marketing Association educates, supports and facilitates networking among authors, publishers, speakers, trainers, coaches, and consultants, and publishes Dan Kennedy's *No B.S. Info-Marketing Letter*. To learn more, visit **www.Info-Marketing.org**.

3. Dan Kennedy's books and information about them can be found at **www.NoBSBooks.com**. The books are available from all booksellers, including **Amazon.com**, **Barnes&Noble.com**, Barnes & Noble, and 1-800-CEO-BOOKS.

4. To contact Dan Kennedy directly concerning consulting/coaching, direct-response copywriting, ghost writing, coauthorship, speaking engagements, or other matters, please fax to 602-269-3113.

Resources & Free Offers

from Adam Witty

1. EMSI Public Relations is a pay-for-performance PR firm that we recommend to authors. They can help authors get print coverage, talk radio interviews, and TV appearances. They will take the time to get to know you, your book, and your ultimate business goals and then craft a plan to meet them. Best of all, you don't pay unless they get results. Learn more at **emsincorporated.com** or call 1-800-881-7342.

2. Gonzalez & Oberlander LLP is the intellectual property firm that we recommend to authors. Carol Desmond, intellectual property specialist at GO is the go-to-gal for authors that want to protect the IP associated with their book. Visit **golawny.com** or contact Carol directly at cdesmond@golawny.com or call 914-220-5474.

3. Craig Simpson is *the* master direct mail consultant we recommend to authors. Craig specializes in developing direct mail campaigns to support new customer acquisition and backend profits, all while coaching you on how to achieve unheard of ROIs from direct mail. Visit **Simpson-Direct.com** or contact Craig directly at craig@simpson-direct.com or call 541-956-2160.

4. Advantage Media Group, an international publisher of business, self-improvement and professional development books and online learning, offers a suite of book writing, book publishing and book marketing services. If you are ready to take the first and most important step toward becoming a published author and reap the benefits of authorship for your business, contact us today at advantagefamily.com or call 1-866-775-1696.

Visit **BOOKTHEBUSINESS.COM** to access
these free resources:

 RECEIVE a subscription to the Author Success
University™ monthly teleseminars wherein successful
authors and book marketing experts reveal their tips and
tricks for marketing and growing a business with a book

 REGISTER for a webinar led by Adam Witty:
"How to Quickly Write, Publish, And Profit From
A Book That Will Grow Your Business"

 COMPLETE Advantage's Publishing Questionnaire and
receive a complimentary Discovery Consultation with an
acquisitions editor to help you determine if your ideas,
concepts, or manuscript are worth turning into a book

ACCESS ALL OF THE ABOVE FREE RESOURCES
BY REGISTERING YOUR BOOK AT
BOOKTHEBUSINESS.COM

About the Authors

Dan Kennedy is a strategic advisor, consultant, freelance direct-response copywriter, business coach, editor of six business newsletters, and a popular professional speaker as well as a multimillionaire, serial entrepreneur. He directly influences more than one million business owners annually. He is also a thought-leader in the information-marketing field, with clients operating $1 million to $30 million niche-industry publishing, training, and coaching entities in over 100 fields including chiropractic, dentistry, insurance, financial services, restaurants, retail, real estate, and so on, as well as in mainstream categories such as weight loss, health and wellness, personal development, and entrepreneurship. Each year, he is the featured speaker at GKIC's annual, international INFO-Summit, the convention of the information marketing industry. He is the author of 21 books, including titles that have graced the *Inc.* magazine list of 100 Best Business Books, and the Amazon and *Business Week* best-seller lists. Rich Karlgaard, the publisher of *Forbes*, favorably compared Dan's nonfiction writing to the writing of famed novelist Thomas Wolfe.

Books Currently in Print by Dan Kennedy

In the No B.S. Series, published by Entrepreneur Press

- *No B.S. Direct Marketing for Non-Direct Marketing Businesses,* 2nd ed.

- *No B.S. Trust-Based Marketing* (with Matt Zagula)
- *No B.S. Guide to Marketing to Leading-Edge Boomers & Seniors* (with Chip Kessler)
- *No B.S. Price Strategy* (with Jason Marrs)
- *No B.S. Marketing to the Affluent*
- *No B.S. Sales Success in the New Economy*
- *No B.S. Business Success in the New Economy*
- *No B.S. Wealth Attraction in the New Economy*
- *No B.S. Ruthless Management of People & Profits*
- *No B.S. Time Management for Entrepreneurs*

From Other Publishers

- *Unfinished Business: My Autobiographical Essays* (Advantage Media Group)
- *Ultimate Sales Letter*, 4th ed./twentieth anniversary ed. (Adams Media)
- *Ultimate Marketing Plan*, 4th ed./twentieth anniversary ed. (Adams Media)
- *Making Them Believe: The 21 Principles & Lost Secrets of Dr. J. R. Brinkley-Style Marketing* (with Chip Kessler) (GKIC/Morgan-James)
- *Make 'Em Laugh & Take Their Money* (GKIC/Morgan-James)
- *The New Psycho-Cybernetics* (with Dr. Maxwell Maltz) (Prentice-Hall)

Others' Books, Dan as Coauthor

- *Uncensored Sales Strategies by Sydney Barrows* (Entrepreneur Press)
- *Secrets of Peak Performers* (Advantage Media Group)
- *Marketing Magic* (Celebrity Press)

ADAM WITTY is the Founder and Chief Executive Officer of Advantage Media Group, an international publisher of business, self-improvement, and professional-development books and online learning. Adam has worked with hundreds of entrepreneurs, business leaders, and professionals to help them write, publish, monetize, and market a book to grow their businesses.

Adam is an in-demand speaker and consultant on marketing and business development techniques for entrepreneurs and authors. He has been featured in the *Wall Street Journal, Investors Business Daily*, and *Fortune* magazine, as well as on ABC and Fox. He was named to the 2011 *Inc.* magazine "30 Under 30" list of America's Coolest Entrepreneurs and has piloted Advantage Media Group to the 2012 and 2013 Inc 500|5000 list of fastest growing private companies in America. In 2012 the Chilean government selected Adam to judge the prestigious Start-up Chile! entrepreneurship competition. Adam is the Vice Chair of the Board of Directors of Youth Entrepreneurship South Carolina and serves on the board of Clemson University's Spiro Institute for Entrepreneurial Leadership. Mr. Witty can be reached at 843-414-5600 or awitty@advantageww.com.

Books Currently in Print by Adam Witty

- *21 Ways to Build Your Business with a Book* (Advantage Media Group)
- *The Book Itch: Is There a Book in You?* (with Allen Fahden) (Advantage Media Group)
- *Log On and Learn: How to Quickly and Easily Create Online Courses That Expand Your Brand, Cultivate Customers, and Make You Money While You Sleep* (Advantage Media Group)
- *11 Ways Financial Advisors Attract Their Ideal Clients with a Book: How to Stand Out in a Crowded Market and Dramatically Differ-*

entiate Yourself as the Authority, Celebrity and Expert (Advantage Media Group)

- *21 Ways to Build Your Dental Practice With a Book: How To Stand Out In A Crowded Market And Dramatically Differentiate Yourself As The Authority, Celebrity and Expert* (Advantage Media Group)